The position of aliens in relation to the European Convention on Human Rights

Hélène Lambert

Council of Europe Publishing

French edition:

*La situation des étrangers au regard de la Convention européenne
des Droits de l'Homme*

ISBN: 978-92-871-6155-0

The author acknowledges the many contributions made by Andrew Drzemczewski in the first edition, which are included in this third edition.

Cover design: Graphic Design Workshop, Council of Europe
Layout: Ogham/Harald Mourreau

Council of Europe Publishing
http//book.coe.int
F-67075 Strasbourg Cedex

This book has also been published in the Human rights files series, No. 8

ISBN: 978-92-871-6098-0 Third Edition
© Council of Europe, December 2006
Printed at the Council of Europe

Contents

Preface

The law of the European Convention on Human Rights relating to aliens has grown significantly over the last twenty years. The Council of Europe now comprises 46 members, including Bosnia and Herzegovina, Serbia and Monaco as the last three countries to have joined the Organisation on 24 April 2002, 3 April 2003 and 5 October 2004, respectively.[1] All 46 members have ratified the European Convention on Human Rights (Monaco being the last country to have done so on 30 November 2005). Supplementary rights and freedoms to those guaranteed in the European Convention on Human Rights[2] are provided in Protocols Nos. 1, 4, 6, 7 and 13.[3] Of significance is Protocol No. 12 (opened for signature on 4 November 2000) which entered into force on 1 April 2005. This protocol enlarges the non-discrimination clause contained in Article 14 of the European Convention on Human Rights to "any rights set forth by law". In addition, Protocol No. 11 has reformed the Strasbourg enforcement institutions and mechanisms in order to accommodate the increasing case-load of the Strasbourg institutions.[4] Further major amendments are foreseen by Protocol No. 14 (opened for signature on 13 May 2005; not yet in force) to improve the effective operation of the European Court of Human Rights faced with an ever-increasing volume of applications. Finally, since 11 September 2001, the struggle against terrorism has not always been conducted with full respect for human rights standards. It is against this background that the "Position of Aliens in Relation to the European Convention on Human Rights" is re-examined in a third edition of this publication.

1. Introduction

Traditionally the treatment of aliens has been regulated by the law of state responsibility, in particular, the "international minimum standards" of fundamental justice to be found in customary international law and the standard of "national treatment" (i.e., a state is only required to provide aliens and nationals with equal treatment, not with any special treatment).[5] More recently, this treatment has come to be measured against a new and higher set of international standards to be found in human rights law.[6] Two important consequences result from this new approach. Firstly, the doctrine of equality (of treatment) has given rise to the principle of non-discrimination which imposes strict limitations upon the freedom of states to deal with aliens.[7] Secondly, *all* human beings have become subjects of modern international law to the extent that human rights treaties grant rights to individuals that they may enforce directly before an international body, without a link of nationality.[8] The traditional rules of the law of state responsibility remain nevertheless applicable to the treatment of aliens in countries which are not parties to or have made important reservations to the basic human rights treaties, and on the matter of remedies.

This study examines the standards of treatment afforded to aliens under the European Convention on Human Rights (hereinafter the ECHR). It is divided into two main sections. Section 1 looks at the general background concerning the position of aliens in international law. Following a general discussion on the ECHR (1.A), this section considers the rights and duties of states towards aliens under general international law in the context of admission and expulsion (1.B) and non-discrimination (1.C). Section 2 specifically concentrates on the rights and freedoms of aliens under the ECHR. Following some general observations (2.A), this section examines the concept of alienage under specific provisions of the ECHR (2.B) as well as in Strasbourg's case law (2.C).

A. General observations

The European Convention on Human Rights as a treaty with particular characteristics

Unlike other treaties of international law, the ECHR is not subject to the traditional doctrines of "reciprocity" and "nationality".[9] The European Court of Human Rights (hereinafter the Court) rejected the doctrine of reciprocity in the case of *Ireland v. the United Kingdom*, when it stated:

unlike international treaties of the classic kind, the Convention comprises more than mere reciprocal engagements between contracting States. It creates, over and above a network of mutual, bilateral undertakings, objective obligations, which in the words of the Preamble, benefit from a "collective enforcement".[10]

This was already the view of the International Court of Justice in *Barcelona Traction, Light and Power Company, Limited (Belgium v. Spain)* when it stated:

> 33. ... an essential distinction should be drawn between the obligations of a State towards the international community as a whole, and those arising *vis-à-vis* another State in the field of diplomatic protection. By their very nature the former are the concern of all States. In view of the importance of the rights involved, all States can be held to have a legal interest in their protection; they are obligations *erga omnes*.

> 34. Such obligations derive, for example, in contemporary international law, from the outlawing of acts of aggression, and of genocide, as also from the principles and rules concerning basic rights of the human person including protection from slavery and racial discrimination.[11]

More recently, the Court has referred to the ECHR as "a constitutional instrument of European public order *(ordre public)*".[12] The ECHR does not recognise the doctrine of "nationality" either. As stated by Higgins, "[h]uman rights are rights held simply by virtue of being a human person".[13] According to Article 1 ECHR, "everyone" within the jurisdiction of a contracting party benefits from the rights and freedoms enumerated in the ECHR. This means that, in theory at least, the rights and freedoms recognised by the ECHR are universally available to all individuals, including aliens, be they nationals (e.g., immigrants or refugees) or non-nationals (e.g., stateless) of a foreign state. It follows that considerations of nationality, residence or domicile are irrelevant to a determination of a claim of a violation of the ECHR. All that needs to be shown is some physical presence in the territory of the (alleged) violator contracting party,[14] and some exercise of control by that state over the individual and over the protection of the ECHR's rights secured within the territory of the state.[15]

In the context of return, the Court further recognised the extraterritoriality effect of provisions of the ECHR, in particular Article 3, when it held that a contracting party could be held responsible for treatment afforded to a person within a non-contracting party to the ECHR in the context of extradition (but also expulsion, deportation, etc.) procedures.[16] Extraterritoriality, though a controversial issue in public international law, has nevertheless been accepted in the context of a treaty rule recognising a rule of customary international law,[17] and the *non-refoulement* principle may be claimed to be part of this body of customary rules.[18] The Court has nonetheless restricted the recognition of this extraterritorial legal space to the exceptional, thereby reaffirming the essentially territorial notion of the concept of juris-diction under Article 1 ECHR.[19]

The ECHR embodies many of the rights and freedoms covered in the Universal Declaration of Human Rights (1948). However, it contains mostly civil and political rights, leaving the bulk of economic, social and cultural rights to be protected under the European Social Charter and/or the International Covenant on Economic, Social and Cultural Rights.[20] Thus, provisions concerning, for instance, ownership of property, freedom of movement or a right of asylum were left out from the contents of the ECHR. Various protocols have since extended the scope of these rights and freedoms. For instance, the protection of property and the right to education became protected under Protocol No. 1 (Articles 1 and 2), and freedom of movement under Protocol No. 4 (Article 2). This is not the case of the right of asylum, which remains outside the ambit of the ECHR and its protocols. Many States Parties to the ECHR have not, however, ratified the protocols.[21]

Besides rights and freedoms, the ECHR also provides guarantees aimed at reinforcing the efficacy of these rights and freedoms. For instance, Article 13 provides the right to an effective remedy. Article 14 guarantees the enjoyment of the rights and freedoms contained in the ECHR without discrimination on any ground such as sex, race, colour, language, religion, political or other opinion, national or social origin, association with a national minority, property, birth or other status.[22] Protocol No. 12 broadens the field of application of Article 14 to include "the enjoyment of any right specifically granted to an individual under national law" against discrimination by public authorities. Exceptions to the non-discrimination clause in Article 14 and Article 1 of Protocol No. 12 are contemplated under the ECHR in the light of the following provisions:

- Article 57, according to which states may "make a reservation in respect of any particular provision of the Convention";

- Article 15, allowing states to take measures derogating from their obligations under the ECHR; such measures must be limited to the "extent strictly required by the exigencies of the situation" and may not be made against Articles 2, 3, 4 (1), or 7 of the ECHR or against rights provided in Protocol No. 6 and Protocol No. 13;[23]

- Article 16, according to which states may restrict the political activities of aliens in connection to their rights under Articles 10, 11 and 14 (and now also Article 1, Protocol No. 12);

- Qualified rights (for example, by the engagement of other rights, or by the needs of society, e.g., Articles 8-11) or limited rights (i.e., only in defined circumstances and ways, e.g., Articles 5 and 6), according to which states are entitled to restrict the enjoyment of these rights on the ground of concepts to be defined by the states (e.g., necessary in a democratic society, in the interest of the community, with a view to deportation);

- Finally, considerations of necessity and proportionality which have sometimes required the Strasbourg organs to allow a differentiation to be made.[24]

The Strasbourg enforcement machinery

According to the ECHR, the primary responsibility for implementing the rights and freedoms guaranteed therein rests with the Contracting Parties, "the machinery of protection established by the Convention is subsidiary to the national systems safeguarding human rights".[25] The Strasbourg organs have nevertheless played a crucial role in the enforcement of these rights. The Court has repeatedly "emphasised that the Convention is a living instrument to be interpreted in the light of present-day conditions and this approach applies not only to the substantive rights protected under the Convention, but also to those provisions which govern the operation of the Convention's enforcement machinery".[26] Not too long ago, the Court expressed "the view that the *increasingly high standard* being required in the area of protection of human rights and fundamental liberties correspondingly and inevitably requires greater firmness in assessing breaches of the fundamental values of democratic societies" (emphasis added).[27] In addition, the Court has developed the principle of effective and practical protection through a constant enlargement of the positive obligations of states when implementing the rights and freedoms guaranteed under the ECHR. For instance, the Court found that the prohibition against torture, inhuman or degrading treatment under Article 3 requires two types of states behaviour on the part of states: they must abstain from such treatment and they must take immediate steps to prevent, prosecute and punish the authors of such acts (and in particular, they must allow the victim effective access to the procedure of investigation).[28] It follows from this approach that a state could be found responsible for a violation of the ECHR following the violation of a substantive and/or procedural component of any right or freedom guaranteed under the ECHR.[29]

Since the entry into force of Protocol No. 11 on 1 November 1998, the new Court has become a full-time institution (Article 19) and its jurisdiction compulsory for contracting states (Article 32).[30] All individuals have gained direct access to the new Court and "The Contracting Parties undertake not to hinder in any way the effective exercise of this right" (Article 34). Inter-state applications (Article 33) continue to be rare, however, and motivated by considerations of self-interest and politics, in spite of the fact that "[u]nlike the traditional approach to such cases under the international law of state responsibility for injury to aliens, it is not necessary for an applicant state to allege that the rights of its own nationals have been violated".[31] This lack of states' motivation is highly regrettable for the treatment of aliens in Europe, in particular the stateless. Judgments of the Court are legally binding and their execution is supervised by the Committee of Ministers.[32]

The Council of Europe is now composed of 46 member states, of which almost half are newly constituted republics resulting from the collapse of former communist regimes. All 46 member states have signed and ratified the ECHR, Monaco being the last one to have done so on 30 November 2005. Mahoney sees the changed character of contracting parties as constituting a serious challenge for the Court. Not least, the principle upon which the Court is only empowered to review the exercise of democratic discretion by national authorities (i.e., subsidiarity) has become subject to serious undermining. He predicts, in particular, that in future the new Court is likely to become increasingly involved in cases of blatant and serious violations of human rights (e.g., Article 2 or 3) as opposed to cases involving the margin of appreciation (e.g., Articles 8-11).[33]

Whilst Protocol No. 11 aimed mostly at enhancing the accessibility and visibility of the Court and at reinforcing the judicial character of the control system provided by the ECHR, it failed to address the problem of the Court's excessive case-load. Thus, a new additional Protocol No. 14 was opened for signature on 13 May 2005 (not yet ratified), aiming at enhancing the effective operation of the Court, in particular through the introduction of a filtering system, a simplified summary procedure for repetitive cases, and a new admissibility requirement.[34]

B. Rights and duties of states towards the admission and expulsion of aliens under international law

It has long been a principle of international customary law that states are free to control the entry and residence of aliens. The absence of any duty to admit aliens in classical international law is supported by the practice and immigration laws of most states, and finds its origins in the principle of sovereignty or territorial supremacy.[35] However, this freedom has come to be increasingly limited under contemporary international law, in particular by treaties and principles of general international law in the areas of human rights and economic integration.[36] Thus, the Treaty on European Union recognises freedom of movement and the right of establishment (e.g., the right to reside and work, and the right to vote and stand as candidates in local and European elections) to all European citizens within the member states of the Union,[37] and freedom of movement is progressively extended to third-country nationals.[38] Aliens are also expressly guaranteed freedom of movement, including the right to emigrate and the right to move freely within a state's territory, under several international treaties of human rights.[39] This freedom is provided, for instance, in Article 13 of the Universal Declaration of Human Rights and Article 12 of the International Covenant on Civil and Political Rights. It is also provided for in Article 2 of Protocol No. 4 to the ECHR.[40]

However, such express guarantees on freedom of movement have never extended to the "right" to immigrate to a country other than one's own, including the right to asylum, which remains governed primarily by national legislation. Certain categories of people are nevertheless either exempt from control on entry or enjoy privileges when seeking entry into a foreign state's territory. This is the case, for instance, of diplomats and consuls, on the basis of customary international law subsequently codified into treaties; of special missions, on the basis of "modern rules of international law" subsequently codified in treaty law; of international officials, on the basis of treaties; and, finally, of crew members, on the basis of bilateral then multilateral treaties.[41] Outside the scope of treaty obligations, states have chosen to admit aliens into their territory for humanitarian motives, albeit on a discrimination basis (e.g., during the Bosnian war, European countries were imposing visa requirements on persons fleeing certain areas of the former Yugoslavia).

Alongside the rights and duties of states regarding the admission of aliens, states are generally recognised the power to remove aliens as part of their territorial sovereignty.[42] In return, the state of the nationality of the alien has a duty to receive him/her back into its territory.[43] This is because in international law, nationality produces two effects: "a state may protect its nationals *vis-à-vis* other states, and it has a duty to readmit them to its territory should another state decide to expel them".[44]

In a series of cases the (permanent) Court of International Justice clarified the notion of states' discretionary power to admit and remove aliens and concluded that such power exists within the rule of law (i.e., the international rules relating to nationality and to human rights) and does not therefore equate to arbitrariness.[45] In particular, such power must be exercised within the rule of law, i.e., it must be in conformity with basic standards, such as fairness and non-discrimination, and it must not clash with other individuals' basic human rights, such as family reunion, *non-refoulement*, and prohibition of torture or degrading treatment. It follows that recent practices aimed at preventing entry or at denying access to the full-length asylum procedures to entire groups of refugees into Europe may raise concern in the light of the principle of non-discrimination.[46] States are required to interpret the Convention Relating to the Status of Refugees in "good faith", and many such practices may not even have a legitimate aim nor meet the proportionality test.[47] More specifically, mass expulsion of aliens is unlawful under Article 4 of Protocol No. 4, and certain procedural rights are guaranteed under Article 1 of Protocol No. 7. Furthermore, matters of expulsion may indirectly raise an issue under Article 3 (prohibition of torture and other ill-treatment), Article 5 (right to liberty and security pending deportation), Article 8 (right to respect for private and family life), and Article 13 (right to an effective remedy), in particular.

Thus, in the absence of general international law and treaty obligations, a state is free to admit or expel an alien from its territory. However, as observed by Goodwin-Gill, this is rarely the case.[48] Human rights treaties, including specific treaties on refugee rights, have considerably narrowed down the margin of discretion belonging to states. In this regard the ECHR has played a key-role *vis-à-vis* European governments.

C. Non-discrimination

Under classical international law, a state is required to respect the basic human rights of its citizens and to accord to all people within its jurisdiction equal protection of their basic human rights without distinction as to race, sex, language or religion.[49] This duty of states is reiterated in several other international instruments.[50] It follows that as a matter of general international law, nothing prevents a state from treating its own nationals better than aliens, provided the "international minimum standard" required in respect of aliens is met. Classical international law does not therefore prevent discrimination by states between aliens and nationals on grounds of nationality. This approach was rejected mostly in human rights treaties of regional character.[51]

It was first rejected by the founding fathers of the Council of Europe and the drafters of the ECHR. Article 14 of the ECHR requires that each of the rights and freedoms guaranteed therein "be secured without discrimination [*sans distinction aucune*] on any ground such as sex, race, colour, language, religion, political or other opinion, national or social origin, association with a national minority, property, birth or other status".[52] Although the scope of application of Article 14 is limited to the way in which states guarantee the rights and freedoms defined in the ECHR, and not any other rights, it does not require an actual violation of a substantive provision.[53] For instance, in *Abdulaziz, Cabales and Balkandali v. the United Kingdom* (a case involving non-national wives granted indefinite leave to remain in the United Kingdom who where seeking the right to be joined there by their non-national husbands), the Court indicated that the British immigration rules applicable at the time did not per se violate Article 8, but since the right sought by the applicants could only be exercised by men, a violation of Article 14 had occurred.[54] Thus, the provisions of the ECHR are principally applicable without any distinction between nationals and aliens within any given member state; alienage per se is generally not a permissible ground for different treatment.[55] However, Article 14 does not require absolute equality or identity in treatment in every situation, and factual inequalities may exceptionally call for legal inequalities in the form of special measures, but only on the basis of an explicit provision in the ECHR allowing for such a differentiation (e.g., Articles 57, 15, 16, 8-11, 5 or 6). For the purpose of the ECHR, a difference of treatment is discriminatory if it "has no objective and reasonable justification", i.e., if it does not pursue "a legitimate aim" or if there is no "reasonable relationship of proportionality between the means employed and the aim sought to be realised".[56] In *Abdulaziz, Cabales and Balkandali v. the United Kingdom,* for instance, the applicants were able to show that the reason advanced by the UK government for distinguishing between men and women, that they had a different effect on the labour market, was without factual basis.[57] In the more recent case of *Koua Poirrez v. France*, the Court found a violation of Article 14 (in relation to Article 1 of Protocol No. 1) on the ground that "the difference in treatment regarding entitlement to social benefits between nationals or nationals of a country having signed a reciprocity agreement and other foreign nationals was not based on any 'objective and reasonable justification'".[58] The Court re-emphasised that contracting states when ratifying the ECHR undertook to "secure to everyone within their jurisdiction the rights and freedoms" in the ECHR. And in *Timishev v. Russia,* having established that discrimination on account of one's actual or perceived ethnicity is a form of racial discrimination, the Court ruled that "no difference in treatment which is based exclusively or to a decisive extent on a person's ethnic origin is capable of being objectively justified in a contemporary democratic society built on the principles of pluralism and respect for different cultures".[59] And it found a violation of Article 14 in conjunction with Article 2 of Protocol No. 4.

Thus, non-discrimination is not guaranteed in absolute terms in the ECHR. The contracting parties enjoy "a certain margin of appreciation in assessing whether and to what extent differences in otherwise similar situations justify a different treatment in law, but it is for the Court to give the final ruling in this respect".[60] If no justification for the different treatment is offered by the state, the applicant will usually succeed.[61] So will s/he, when a proper balance is not achieved between the interests involved and when the means employed are therefore disproportionate to the legitimate aim pursued.[62]

Protection against discrimination under Article 14 of the ECHR was recently complemented by additional Protocol No. 12. This protocol entered into force on 1 April 2005 and has only been ratified by 13 contracting parties to the ECHR so far.[63] Protocol No. 12 broadens the scope of the application of Article 14 ECHR by providing a complete autonomous application of the principle of non-discrimination "to any right set forth by law" (in particular, national law).[64] More specifically, Protocol No. 12 enlarges the scope of protection against non-discrimination to include a negative obligation for the contracting parties (the obligation not to discriminate against individuals) as well as a positive obligation (to take measures to prevent discrimination, even where discrimination occurs between private parties).[65] It sits next to Article 14 ECHR without amending it or abrogating it. However, like Article 14 ECHR, Protocol No. 12 does not guarantee non-discrimination in absolute terms. Rather it follows the approach adopted by the Court in its case law (i.e., not every difference of treatment amounts to discrimination and a certain margin of appreciation is recognised to national authorities in assessing whether and to what extent differences in otherwise similar situations justify a different treatment in law). Nonetheless, this case law shows that the Court has been able to control states' freedom in the area of immigration, residence, and integration of aliens through a generous application of the principle of proportionality and a liberal interpretation of provisions of the ECHR.[66] Protocol No. 12 thus allows the door to open to individual cases arguing that differential treatment between nationals and foreigners for instance regarding social rights is not objectively and reasonably justified.

The traditional approach to non-discrimination in international law was also rejected in other fora. The International Court of Justice endorsed the new approach in the *Barcelona Traction* case, arguing that such a view was justified on the basis of "principles and rules concerning basic rights of the human persons".[67] Article 24 of the American Convention on Human Rights generally recognises to "all persons" equal protection of the law "without discrimination", and Article 3 of the Additional Protocol ("of San Salvadore") in the area of economic, social and cultural rights is more explicit in providing "national ... origin ... or any other social condition" as a basis for non-discrimination. In Africa, Article 2 of the African Charter on Human and Peoples' Rights explicitly mentions "national ... origin ... or other status" as grounds for non-discrimination. Within the European Union discriminatory treatment on the basis of nationality is generally prohibited.[68] This general prohibition does not yet fully extend to third-country nationals.[69] It is unquestionable that developments in human rights fora have raised the standards of protection of *all* human beings, aliens and nationals alike. Today, aliens and nationals benefit from non-discriminatory protection of their basic human rights. Henceforth, restrictions imposed on aliens but not on nationals must be expressly stated. When such differential treatment is allowed, it must pursue a legitimate aim (i.e., it must have an objective and reasonable justification) and a reasonable relationship of proportionality must exist between the aims sought to be realised and the means employed.[70] This is also the case concerning the differential treatment of categories of aliens. Exceptionally, such distinction may not only be permissible but also desirable and necessary in any immigration system (e.g., between male and female asylum seekers).[71]

Three key points follow from the above discussion. One, alienage is not a ground for discrimination under the ECHR. Two, restrictions may be imposed on aliens as a matter of exception following an express provision in the ECHR. Against this background aliens are recognised as having specific rights under the ECHR. Three, the system of protection under the ECHR is supplementary to that provided by municipal law and/or other international agreements and may only be resorted to by aliens in order to benefit from a more favourable regime for the protection of their human rights.

2. The scope of the rights and freedoms of aliens under the ECHR

A. General observations

In principle, alienage per se is not a ground for discrimination between aliens and nationals under the ECHR. Yet, the ECHR contains several exceptions to this principle resulting in the exclusion or the particular inclusion of aliens from the enjoyment of some basic human rights. This is the case, in particular of Article 5 (1) *f,* Article 16, Article 1 of Protocol No. 1, Articles 2 (1) and 4 of Protocol No. 4, and Article 1 of Protocol No. 7, which all contain direct limitations on the non-discrimination clause. In addition, Articles 8 to 11 have been found to limit indirectly the non-discrimination clause by allowing states to take restrictive measures justified by the need to accommodate the protection of certain human rights on one hand, and the protection of democratic society on the other hand. This is generally recognised as a function of municipal law and wide discretion is exercised by states in their choice of restrictions. Furthermore, Article 6 of the ECHR has been interpreted by the Court to exclude immigration proceedings. In contrast, the ECHR also provides certain provisions which *prima facie* do not concern aliens but which have been interpreted to benefit them in a special way (e.g., Article 3 in connection with Article 13). This led Lillich to observe that "The European Convention on Human Rights provides a classic example of how, with a bit of imagination, principles relating to the human rights of aliens can be extracted from legal instruments which on their surface seemingly have little or nothing to do with the subject".[72]

B. Alienage and specific provisions of the ECHR

At present, the ECHR contains at least six provisions according to which aliens and nationals may be treated differently. Like all exceptions, they must be interpreted restrictively, that is, they "shall not be applied for any purposes other than those for which they have been prescribed" (Article 18 ECHR), and apart from the exception provided in Article 16 they shall not be applied in a discriminatory way, that is, they are subject to the requirements of necessity and proportionality.

Restrictions on the political activity of aliens

Article 16 of the ECHR[73] provides the first and only explicit exception to the non-discriminatory clause expressed in Article 14, by allowing the contracting parties to impose restrictions on the political activities of aliens in respect of Article 10 ("Freedom of expression"), Article 11 ("Freedom of assembly and association") and Article 14 ("Prohibition of discrimination"). The *travaux préparatoires* suggest that Article 16 was included in the ECHR to reflect the customary international law evidence that states are free to restrict the political activity of aliens.[74] Since then, this provision has been criticised for conflicting with Article 1 of the ECHR (i.e., the enjoyment by everyone of the rights and freedoms guaranteed therein) and for applying to potentially wide provisions such as Article 14.[75] The Parliamentary Assembly of the Council of Europe even called for its deletion in 1977.

The scope of Article 16 was discussed by the Court in *Piermont v. France.*[76] The applicant, a German citizen and a member of the European Parliament (MEP), had been invited to French overseas territories (OTs) in the South Pacific by "green" groups against nuclear tests. In French Polynesia she took part in demonstrations against the government and was expelled from the territory with prohibition on re-entering. She claimed that the measure violated her freedom of expression under Article 10. The French Government argued that, if not justified under other grounds (e.g., Article 56), the measure could at least fall under the scope of Article 16. The Court disagreed and found, in favour of the applicant, that her "possession of the nationality of a member State of the European Union and, in addition to that, her status as a member of the European Parliament do not allow Article 16 of the Convention to be raised against her, especially as the people of the OTs take part in the European Parliament elections".[77] There was great disagreement on the reasons why Mrs Piermont should not be considered an alien for the purposes of her claim. The majority in the Court refused to rely on the concept of citizenship of the European Union because the Community treaties did not at the time recognise any such citizenship. Similarly, it refused to base its decision on her status as an MEP. Instead, it found that, under the Community treaties, citizenship of a *member state* was sufficient to remove the status of alien from the applicant. Thus, European Union nationals present in a member state of the European Union of which they do not have citizenship are not "aliens" for the purposes of Article 16. This interpretation is to be welcomed for it provides the Court with an opportunity "to control resort to the Article 16 power" otherwise left at the discretion of the contracting parties.[78]

States' power to detain aliens

The second exception is contained in Article 5 (1) *f* of the ECHR, which recognises the power of states to detain (aliens) in order to prevent unauthorised entry or with a view to deportation or extradition. The Court's case law shows that it is difficult for aliens to invoke successfully Article 5 in respect of expulsion or refusal to grant a residence permit in a state.

Article 5 is concerned with the legality of the "deprivation" of liberty,[79] not with the restrictions or limitations on freedom of movement covered by Article 2 of Protocol No. 4 or the legality of the conditions of detention, which is a matter for Article 3 of the ECHR and/or the European Convention for the Prevention of Torture and Inhuman or Degrading Treatment or Punishment.

Article 5 (1) guarantees to everyone the right to physical liberty. This right may be limited on six grounds explicitly listed in Article 5 (1) *a-f.* It follows that under the ECHR, detention is generally presumed to be arbitrary unless it falls under one of the six grounds listed.[80] One such ground is especially relevant in the context of this section because it applies only to aliens, i.e., Article 5 (1) *f*.[81] States' power to detain aliens is not unlimited: in particular, it is subject to three key principles. These principles were discussed by the Court in the context of immigration in *Amuur v. France,* a case involving four sibling asylumseekers from Somalia held in the international zone of Paris Orly airport for twenty days.[82] They are summarised as follows:

- Whether the detention in question amounts to a deprivation or a restriction upon liberty is a question of degree or intensity, and not one of nature or substance.[83] In its assessment of this degree, the Court looks at each concrete situation, i.e., it looks at the type, duration, effects and manner of implementation of the measure. Thus, the ECHR does not confer a right of political asylum or, more generally, a right of residence.[84] However, "the confinement must not deprive the asylum-seeker of the right to gain effective access to the procedure for determining refugee status".[85]

- Once the Court is convinced that it is dealing with a deprivation of liberty, it moves on to establish the legality of the detention, i.e., whether it is "in accordance with a procedure prescribed by law". The Court has interpreted this requirement to mean that the domestic law authorising the deprivation of liberty "must be sufficiently accessible and precise, in order to avoid all risk of arbitrariness".[86] It must also be of "sufficient quality", i.e., it must offer possibilities for judicial review, provisions setting time limits and access to legal, humanitarian and social assistance.[87]

- The deprivation of liberty must be "necessary in a democratic society". In particular, it must "be in conformity with the purpose" of the limitation.[88] Such purpose includes the prevention of unlawful immigration or of a real risk of absconding. In such cases, account should be taken of the distinction between aliens who are not suspected criminals and others who are suspected criminals.[89] In *Chahal v. the United Kingdom,* a case of deportation to India of a Sikh separatist on grounds of national security, the Court distinguished the requirement of "necessity" under Article 5 (1) *f* from that under Article 5 (1) *c,* and it found that Article 5 (1) *f* did not require that the detention of an alien against whom action was being taken with a view to deportation be reasonably considered necessary. All that was required was that "action is being taken with a view to deportation".[90] Thus, detention would be justified even if a deportation order had not yet been in force. However, it would cease to be justified if the deportation proceedings were to be conducted without due diligence.[91] It was therefore necessary for the Court to determine whether the duration of the deportation proceedings was excessive and whether there existed sufficient guarantees against arbitrariness. The Court found a period of almost four years, during which Mr Chahal's application for asylum was being considered, not to be excessive in view of the seriousness of the interest involved, i.e., Mr Chahal's fear of torture balanced against the national security of the country.[92] It also found that in the context of Article 5 (1), the advisory panel procedure provided in cases of national security offered sufficient guarantees against arbitrariness.[93] In the recent case of *Saadi v. the United Kingdom*, the Court was considering an application from an Iraqi citizen who had claimed asylum upon arrival in the United Kingdom.[94] He was granted temporary admission and four days later was detained for seven days. The Court agreed with the government that "until a potential immigrant has been granted leave to remain in the country, he has not effected a lawful entry, and detention can reasonably be considered to be aimed at preventing unlawful entry".[95] The Court further agreed that such detention was permissible even in circumstances where there is no risk of his absconding or other misconduct. This is because in the context of Article 5 (1) *f,* dealing in particular with potential immigrants, the state has a broader discretion than when dealing with other interferences with the right to liberty, i.e., the detention does not need to be "reasonably considered necessary". And the Court concluded that since the detention had lasted only seven days, no violation of Article 5 (1) *f* had occurred.[96]

Article 5 (2)-(5) sets out a number of safeguards in respect of anyone who is lawfully detained.[97] Under Article 5 (2), anyone arrested must be "informed promptly" and in a language that s/he understands of the reasons why s/he was arrested, so as to be able to seek judicial review of his/her arrest or detention under Article 5 (4).[98] Thus, in *Zamir v. the United Kingdom*, the Commission was of the opinion that free legal aid should have been made available to an illegal immigrant detained pending deportation because of his poor command of English and the complexity of the case.[99] Article 5 (3) contains important safeguards for anyone arrested or detained on suspicion of having committed a criminal offence under Article 5 (1) *c.*[100] Article 5 (4) guarantees to everyone who is "lawfully" detained under Article 5 the right to seek judicial review of their detention "speedily before a court". This provision applies to "everyone", whatever the grounds for detention (e.g., criminal offence or deportation in immigration or asylum cases). The requirement of speediness is particularly important in cases where detention has been ordered by an administrative body. Both access to judicial review and the decision of the review court must be "speedy". Thus, in *Zamir v. the*

United Kingdom, the Commission considered that an application for legal aid related to Article 5 (4) must be considered "speedily"; and seven weeks to hear the review case was found to be in violation for this reason.[101] Periods of thirty-one and forty-six days for a municipal court to review a case were considered in breach of Article 5 (4) in case of detention pending extradition under Article 5 (1) *f.*[102] The requirement of "lawfulness" of the detention under Article 5 (4) has the same meaning as under Article 5 (1), i.e., the detainee must be able to question the conformity of his/her detention with provisions of municipal law and the ECHR, and its arbitrariness.[103] However, Article 5 (4) does not go so far as to require "that the domestic courts should have the power to review whether the underlying decision to expel could be justified under national or Convention law".[104] This does not mean that the national authorities can be free from effective control by the domestic courts whenever elements of national security or terrorism are involved.[105] Thus, in *Chahal v. the United Kingdom*, the Court found that the advisory panel competent to review national security cases fell short of being considered a "court" since it offered no opportunity of legal representation, it had no power of decision, and its advice to the Home Secretary was not binding and could not be disclosed.[106] And in *Al-Nashif v. Bulgaria*, the Court found that the total absence in Bulgarian law of a possibility of judicial appeal in cases of detention pending deportation, where the deportation order is issued on grounds of national security, was in plain violation of Article 5(4).[107] Thus, a state must provide speedy access to a court in all cases, whether the detention is justified under Article 5 (1) *a-f* or not, as confirmed by the Court's jurisprudence that paragraphs (1) and (4) of Article 5 are separate provisions.[108] Article 5 (4) is a more specific and restrictive provision than Article 13 on the "right to an effective remedy"; thus, once a violation of Article 5 (4) is found, the Court does not normally find it necessary to consider a claim under Article 13 in relation to Article 5.[109] This is because both provisions serve the same purpose, i.e., to provide a domestic remedy which would be more easily and quickly attainable under domestic law than at the Strasbourg level. Finally, Article 5 (5) guarantees a right to compensation from the national authorities for unlawful detention.[110] This right is distinct from the right to just satisfaction from the Court under Article 41 in connection with a breach of Article 5.

To sum up, detention for the purpose of refusing entry into the territory, removing an illegal entrant or deporting an alien is permitted under the ECHR in order to accommodate states in the exercise of their power to control immigration. And the Court has recognised a particularly wide margin of discretion for states in respect of Article 5 (1) *f.* Even so, judicial review of the legality of the detention must be guaranteed as a safeguard against the arbitrariness of the measure, including the domestic law upon which it is based. It follows that "a blanket policy of detaining all asylum-seekers on arrival would be incompatible with the ECHR".[111] So would a prolonged detention pending examination of an asylum claim in the absence of a specific reason such as threat to the national security. Furthermore, "Article 5 combined with Article 14 would preclude with selective detention of particular ethnic sub-groups solely on the basis of their race, religion or national origin".[112]

Freedom of movement of aliens lawfully within the territory

The third exception is provided in Article 2 (1) of Protocol No. 4 to the ECHR stating that: "Everyone lawfully (*régulièrement*) within the territory of a State shall, within that territory, have the right to liberty of movement and freedom to choose his residence", subject to the limitations or restrictions applicable to "everyone" provided in Article 2 (3) and (4).[113] Article 2 (1) of Protocol No. 4 clearly only concerns the free movement of persons *within* (as opposed to between) the states parties to the protocol. With the exception of Andorra, Greece, Spain, Switzerland, Turkey and the United Kingdom, all other states that are parties to the ECHR are also parties to Protocol No. 4.[114] Although Article 2 of Protocol No. 4 does not expressly refer to aliens, it has the effect of distinguishing between "everyone lawfully" in a state, who may either be nationals or aliens, and "everyone unlawfully" in a state, who may only be aliens. Consequently, aliens lawfully in a state may move freely within that state and may choose their place of residence, but aliens unlawfully (*en situation irrégulière*) in a state have no such right. The Commission considers that "lawfully" refers to the domestic law of the state in question, and that aliens admitted under certain conditions by the state's authorities are "lawfully within the territory" as long as they comply with those conditions.[115] Thus, persons authorised entry in a country and allowed to remain for a limited time on humanitarian grounds may not necessarily derive a right of permanent admission from their temporary situation.[116] It was also agreed that the scope of Article 2 (1) of Protocol No. 4 would not extend to an alien passing through the territory of a state.[117]

Prohibition of collective expulsion of aliens

The fourth exception applies explicitly to aliens and is provided in Article 4 of Protocol No. 4: "Collective expulsion of aliens is prohibited". Originally inspired by the massive expulsion of peoples as a result of the second world war, Article 4 no longer requires that expulsion be on a massive scale to be collective. In *Becker v. Denmark*, the Commission defined collective expulsion as "any measure of the competent authority compelling aliens as a group to leave the country".[118] These words have been read to mean that "acts of persecution, violations of human rights, discriminatory treatment", etc., at the hand of state authorities or, if at the hands of non-state agents, against which the state cannot or will not offer protection, constitute collective expulsion.[119] However, the refusal of asylum in identical terms to a number of aliens from the same country does not amount to collective expulsion if each of them had his/her asylum application decided on its individual merits. This follows from the Commission's finding in *Becker v. Denmark* that aliens may only be expelled as a group following "a reasonable and objective examination of the particular cases of each individual alien of the group".[121] More recently, the Court endorsed the Commission's definition of collective expulsion to mean "any measure compelling aliens, as a group, to leave a country, except where such a measure is taken on the basis of a reasonable and objective examination of the particular case of each individual alien of the group".[122] And in *Čonka v. Belgium*, the Court found a violation of Article 4 of Protocol No. 4 because the expulsion procedure lacked "sufficient guarantees demonstrating that the personal circumstances of each of those concerned had been genuinely and individually taken into account.[123] Finally, the procedural guarantee under Article 4 of Protocol No. 4 applies generally to all aliens, whether lawfully or unlawfully in the territory of a state, whether resident or non-resident in the territory of that state, whether or not part of a collective group.

Procedural safeguards relating to the expulsion of aliens

The fifth exception is contained in Article 1 of Protocol No. 7, which guarantees "Procedural safeguards relating to the expulsion of aliens".[124] According to this provision, individual aliens "lawfully resident" in a country may only be expelled pursuant to a decision reached by law, and they must be allowed to submit reasons against their expulsion, to have their case reviewed, and to be represented before the competent authority, except when such expulsion is necessary on grounds of public order or national security. Up until very recently, not a single one of the complaints submitted to the Commission/Court had been successful; most of them having been declared inadmissible on the ground that the applicant could not be said to be in the country "lawfully". In light of this, it has been argued that Article 1 of Protocol No. 7 contains some important weaknesses.[125] First, it fails to discuss the grounds on which an alien may be expelled. Second, it is limited to aliens "lawfully resident" in a state, thereby excluding from its scope aliens at the border who have not passed through immigration, aliens present in a territory on a non-residence basis, and aliens against whom a decision regarding their residence is pending. For instance, in *Voulfovitch and Oulianova v. Sweden*, the Commission considered that the applicants, who had been authorised entry into Sweden on a one-day transit visa, but who remained in Sweden while a decision on their asylum application was being taken, were not "lawfully resident" and therefore could not benefit from Article 1 of Protocol No. 7.[126] Third, the conditions of "lawful residence" are determined by municipal law. Fourth, review of the case is by a "competent authority" which does not need to be independent or to have a power of decision.[127] Fifth, the procedural safeguards guaranteed to the alien may be overridden "in the interests of public order" or for reasons of "national security".[128] Finally, Protocol No. 7 has not yet been ratified by all the members of the Council of Europe. As of 7 July 2006, it remains non-ratified by seven member states, including the United Kingdom, Belgium, Germany and the Netherlands. In sum, Article 1 of Protocol No. 7 allows aliens the right to have their arguments against expulsion heard by the executive but it offers limited guarantee of procedural due process in cases of expulsion. Regrettably, the Court has done nothing to fill the gap through a more liberal interpretation of Article 6 (1).[129] But the Court may well have turned the corner in a judgment of 8 June 2006, *Lupsa v. Romania*.[130] The applicant, who was lawfully resident in Romania, had been deported to Serbia on grounds of national security. The Court recognised that even in cases of national security and urgent deportation, the applicant is entitled to rely on the guarantees contained in Article 1 of Protocol No. 7, after being deported.[131] The Court further reminded that expulsion may only take place "pursuant of a decision reached in accordance with law", i.e., domestic law. And that "law" in this context refers to the "existence of a legal basis in domestic law, but also the quality of the law in question" (i.e., it must be accessible, foreseeable, and protect against arbitrary interferences by the public authorities). Since these particular guarantees were found by the Court to be absent in the context of Article 8 of the ECHR, the Court concluded that there had been a violation of Article 1 of Protocol No. 7.[132]

Protection of property

The sixth and last exception is found in Article 1 of Protocol No. 1.[133] According to paragraph 1 of this provision, "Every natural or legal person is entitled to the peaceful enjoyment of his possessions" and deprivation of one's property is prohibited "except in the public interest and subject to the conditions provided for by law and by the general principles of international law". In addition, contracting states are entitled "to control the use of property in accordance with the general interest or to secure the payment of taxes or other contributions or penalties" (paragraph 2). The Court has found that the right to a peaceful enjoyment of possessions does not entail the right for an alien who owns property in another country to *reside permanently* there in order to use his/her property; restrictions applicable to an alien's right of residence in a country are compatible with Article 1 of Protocol No. 1 provided they are not absolute nor permanent.[134] It thus remains uncertain whether or not Article 1 of Protocol No. 1 guarantees a right of entry into a foreign country (through the granting of a visa for example) to aliens who own property. If such a right were to exist, its scope would nevertheless be limited under Article 1 of Protocol No. 1 itself.

The "general principles of international law" referred to in the second sentence of the first paragraph are those protecting the property of aliens, and aliens alone, against arbitrary expropriation and against nationalisation without compensation.[135] This interpretation was confirmed in *James v. the*

United Kingdom, in which the Court, relying on the *travaux préparatoires*, found that the protection of general international law was restricted to aliens.[136] Thus, in theory, compensation may be more generous for aliens than for nationals. However, the effect of such findings is limited in practice to the unlikely situation where the Court would decide to have recourse to the general principles of international law. In such a case these principles prescribe a specific treatment of aliens' property, and the treatment in question would be different from that provided to nationals at the national level.[137] As revealed by the case law, this is unlikely to be the case. In the very few cases decided by the Court concerning the property of aliens (including those cases where the applicants were companies), the Court decided the issue of deprivation and control of property in the light of the principle of lawfulness (i.e., the domestic law) and/or the general interest of the community or the payment of taxes. For instance, in *Beyeler v. Italy*, the Court found the deprivation of property to be unlawful because of "the element of uncertainty in the statute and the considerable latitude it afforded the authorities".[138] It further found that such interference could not be justified on the ground of national interest and that "Irrespective of the applicant's nationality, such enrichment was incompatible with the requirement of a 'fair balance'".[139] In *Gasus Dosier- und Fördertechnik GmbH v. the Netherlands*, the Court considered the interference to the peaceful enjoyment of property to result from the tax authorities exercising their powers of control under domestic legislation, and that "the most natural approach" was thus "to examine Gasus's complaints under the head of 'securing the payment of taxes', which comes under the rule in the second paragraph of Article 1".[140] Thus, the Court relied on the right of states to "enforce such laws as it deems necessary ... to secure the payment of taxes" (i.e., procedural tax laws), and it found no violation of Article 1 of Protocol No. 1. Similarly, in *AGOSI v. the United Kingdom*, it relied on the right of states "to enforce such laws as it deems necessary to control the use of property in accordance with the general interest", i.e., the procedure for the control of the use in the United Kingdom of gold coins.[141]

In all cases involving Article 1 of Protocol No. 1, the Court examines, first, whether the interference was lawful (i.e., whether the domestic law was sufficiently accessible, precise and foreseeable); second, whether it sought to achieve a legitimate aim; and third, whether the means employed were proportionate to the legitimate aim pursued. As demonstrated by *AGOSI v. the United Kingdom* and *Gasus Dosier*, the Court exercises a limited review of the "general interest" justifying interference (e.g. the procedure regulating the control of the use in the United Kingdom of gold coins, and the procedural tax laws) and seems to be more willing to review the proportionality of the means employed ("as it deems necessary"). In this regard, it recognises that a "fair balance" must be struck between the demands of the community's interest (or general interest) and the interest of the individual. The Court's case law further suggests that it is rarely prepared to interpret "as it deems necessary" restrictively, particularly where the property owner is not a national of the state. As a result, states are permitted a wide margin of discretion in the choice of the means employed and of the community's interest justifying interference. *Beyeler v. Italy* stands out against this trend. This is likely to be because of the particular facts and circumstances surrounding the case: the applicant was an individual, the community's interest of universal culture was at stake, the domestic law was unclear, and the government had acted late and inconsistently. Thus, in spite of the reference to "general principles of international law" in Article 1 of Protocol No. 1, allowing for a more favourable treatment to aliens, the Court has so far been reluctant to decide cases involving aliens on this ground. One can only conclude that as things stand, Article 1 of Protocol No. 1 offers limited scope to aliens.[142]

The Court has nonetheless interpreted widely the concept of "possessions" in the first part of Article 1 of Protocol No. 1. It has emphasised that the concept has an autonomous meaning (i.e., not limited to ownership of physical goods and independent of the formal classification in domestic law). Thus, debts, constituting assets, may also be regarded as "property rights", and thus "possessions" for the purposes of Article 1 of Protocol No. 1. The Court has also held that entitlement to welfare benefits, even under a non-contributory scheme (e.g., such as an allowance for a disability), may constitute a pecuniary right for the purposes of Article 1 of Protocol No. 1. However, in order to establish such a right, the person concerned must satisfy the various statutory conditions set by the law.[143] In this respect, the Court found that the provisions of Article 1 of Protocol No. 1 cannot be interpreted as giving an individual a right to a pension of a particular amount.[144]

It follows from the above discussion that the ECHR contains specific restrictions on admission and expulsion. These restrictions are special sanctions against aliens. They are therefore discriminatory, unless objectively and reasonably justifiable. Notwithstanding Article 1 of Protocol No. 1, Article 4 of Protocol No. 4, Article 1 of Protocol No. 7, and Article 5 of the ECHR, states' power to expel aliens is almost unlimited. It is thus elsewhere in the ECHR that protection of aliens against refusal of entry and/or expulsion must be found. Such protection is crucial for only through a right to live in a particular country will aliens fully enjoy their basic human rights. Several provisions of the ECHR have been interpreted successfully by the Strasbourg organs so as to offer special protection for aliens in a way which had not been foreseen by the drafters of the ECHR or its organs of interpretation (e.g., Articles 8 and 3 in connection with Article 13).

C. Alienage and the Strasbourg case law

The Strasbourg organs have been interpreting certain provisions of the ECHR so as to offer special protection to aliens. Such interpretation has taken place against the background of an absence of a right to live in a particular country, except one's own. This last section examines the scope of these provisions. Rights under the ECHR may be conceptualised as being of three kinds: absolute, qualified or limited.[145] Absolute rights are rights considered so fundamental that no derogation whatsoever may ever apply to them. In other words, once established, no defence may be argued against a breach of such rights. This is the case, in particular, of Articles 2 and 3, considered to be "absolute rights"; but also of Articles 4 (1) and 7.[146] Mahoney recently described a violation of these rights as "bad-faith abuse of governmental power".[147] Other rights and freedoms have their scope qualified or limited under the ECHR, thereby presenting states with an opportunity to limit the scope of the non-discriminatory clause. Qualified rights are rights that are moderated by the operation of other rights or by the needs of society, and for which the contracting states are left a considerable margin of discretion (e.g., Articles 8-11). In Mahoney's words, violations of these rights are described as "good-faith limitations on liberty which nevertheless go beyond what is 'necessary in a democratic society'."[148] Limited rights under the ECHR are rights which can be limited in strictly defined circumstances and ways (e.g., Articles 5-6), and states are generally permitted a lesser margin of discretion when implementing such rights.

Absolute rights

Absolute rights under the ECHR include the right to life (Article 2), the prohibition of torture and inhuman or degrading treatment (Article 3), the prohibition of slavery and servitude (Article 4 (1)), and the prohibition of retroactive offences or penalties (Article 7). Neither Article 4 nor Article 7 has given rise to much case law,[149] and there is nothing to suggest that the Strasbourg organs would consider the position of aliens in relation to these rights to be any different from that of other individuals.[150] Yet, Article 3, and Article 2 to some extent, stand out as exceptions to this rule. In particular, the position of aliens under the ECHR has come to be the subject of increased scrutiny under Article 3 in cases involving expulsion, including cases of police custody. The absolute nature of Article 3 was affirmed on many occasions by the Court in spite of arguments to the contrary by governments. Thus, in *Chahal v. the United Kingdom*, the Court held that: "Article 3 enshrines one of the most fundamental values of democratic society ... even in those circumstances [i.e., terrorist violence], the Convention prohibits in absolute terms torture or inhuman or degrading treatment or punishment, irrespective of the victim's conduct ... Article 3 makes no provision for exceptions and no derogation from it is permissible under Article 15 even in the event of a public emergency".[151] This view, which was that of 12 of the 19 judges deciding *Chahal*, has since been re-affirmed in other judgments, including most recently the judgments of the Grand Chamber in *Öcalan v. Turkey* and in *Ramzy v. the Netherlands* (both decided after 9/11).[152] Also, it has long been the view of the Court that "diplomatic assurances" or "memoranda of understanding" can never release a contracting party from its obligations under the ECHR.[153]

Expulsion of aliens under Articles 2 and 3

The right to life and/or prohibition against torture may be at stake in cases where the direct consequence of a measure of expulsion of an alien entails the violation of Article 2 and/or 3 of the ECHR.[154] This may happen in four situations.[155]

1. The most common situation is where an alien is subject to an expulsion order to a country where "substantial grounds have been shown for believing that s/he would face a real risk of being subject to treatment contrary to Article 3" or of being killed on return in circumstances that amount to a breach of Article 2.[156] This is the test adopted in *Soering v. the United Kingdom*, a case of extradition to a country where the applicant was going to be subjected to the death penalty in the State of Virginia.[157] The Court found that capital punishment per se did not violate the right to life nor that it constituted ill-treatment contrary to Article 3.[158] However, it concluded that in the light of the particular circumstances surrounding the case (i.e., the length of detention prior to execution, the conditions on death row, the age and mental state of the applicant, the possibility of extradition to Germany) "substantial grounds" had been shown that Jens Soering would face a "real risk" of being subjected to treatment contrary to Article 3 if returned to the requesting state.[159] The Court also made it clear that in all such cases it is the responsibility of the sending state which is engaged, never that of the receiving state.[160] The Soering test was extended to situations where an alien is subject to an expulsion order and the treatment to be expected in the country of destination suggests a real and present risk to the life of the applicant other than the risk of being subjected to the death-row phenomenon, e.g., lack of medical care or very extreme poverty. In all such cases, both the Commission and the Court have considered the matter under Article 2 as raising issues "indissociable from the substance" under Article 3, and have chosen to decide the cases under Article 3.[161]

The requirement of "substantial grounds" has been interpreted by the Strasbourg organs to mean that reasonable grounds exist that expulsion is going to take place, i.e., whether the alien is going to be expelled for certain and imminently and whether the country of destination will subject this person to such treatment.[162] In particular, the Court considers that the mere possibility of ill-treatment is not sufficient, and it requires that the individual be singled out from a situation of general violence.[163] It also considers the risk of being sent on to a (first or) third country to be relevant.[164] When considering the element of "real risk", the Court recognises a "real risk" when "the foreseeable consequences" of the contracting party's decision to expel is that the applicant will be subject to treatment contrary to Article 3 in the final country of destination. In assessing such foreseeability, the Court requires a high degree of proof, particularly in cases involving national security or protection of the public good.[165] In cases involving victims of torture, it accepted that "inconsistencies and contradictions in the testimonies of the applicants and their witness" but did not consider that this lack of precision "by itself impinged upon the credibility of the testimony".[166]

Once "substantial grounds" and "real risk" have been shown, ill-treatment must be found to reach a minimum level of severity in order to fall under Article 3. The Court has held that:

> The assessment of this minimum is, in the nature of things, relative; it depends on all the circumstances of the case, such as the nature and the context of the treatment or punishment, the manner and method of its execution, its duration, its physical or mental effects and, in some instances, the sex, age and state of health of the victim.[167]

For the Court, the distinction between degrading treatment and torture proceeds mainly from a difference of intensity in the suffering. In *Ireland v. the United Kingdom*, the Court defined torture as "deliberate inhuman treatment causing very serious and cruel suffering".[168] In the landmark case *Selmouni v. France*, a case of ill-treatment of an alien in police custody, the Court considered Article 1 of the United Nations Convention Against Torture (1984) to be relevant to an assessment of the treatment suffered, in particular the requirements of "severe pain or suffering" and that this pain be "intentionally inflicted".[169] It then took the view that "the increasingly high standard being required in the area of the protection of human rights and fundamental liberties correspondingly and inevitably requires greater firmness in assessing breaches of the fundamental values of democratic societies", of which Article 3 is one of the most fundamental.[170] The Court has not so far referred to "torture" in cases of expulsion; rather it has generally relied on the notion of inhuman or degrading treatment.[171] As Blake notes, "The critical concept must be that of degrading treatment prohibited absolutely by Article 3".[172] It is indeed this concept of degrading treatment (or punishment) that constitutes the "minimum level of severity" necessary to activate Article 3.[173] For the treatment (or punishment) to be inhuman or degrading, the suffering or humiliation involved must attain a particular level and in any event go beyond that inevitable element of suffering or humiliation connected with a given form of legitimate punishment.[174] The Court's case law further shows that degrading treatment, as opposed to inhuman treatment, causes feelings of gross humiliation in the person concerned; it does not need to cause actual physical harm.[175] Thus, in expulsion cases, the Strasbourg organs have recognised the application of Article 3 from the cumulative effect of ill-treatment, which if taken individually would not reach the threshold of severity required by Article 3. For instance, the Commission (prior to its dissolution) reported that confronting alone an illness such as AIDS at an advanced stage would constitute degrading treatment;[176] but it rejected a similar claim because the illness of the applicant was not yet in an advanced stage.[177] In *Tanko v. Finland*, the Commission also accepted that the enforcement of an expulsion order, which would result in subjecting the applicant to a risk of losing his eyesight in view of the inadequate facilities for treating him and possibly operating on him in the country of destination, could in principle constitute a violation of Article 3.[178] And, in *Fadele v. the United Kingdom*, the Commission recognised that extreme poverty and poor living conditions in the country of destination may also raise an issue under Article 3.[179] The Court took a more restrictive line in the landmark case *D. v. the United Kingdom*. In this case, the Court recognised that the expulsion to a country where lack of medical care would have the effect of reducing even further life expectancy of an applicant suffering from AIDS constituted a violation of Article 3. However, it stressed the "very exceptional circumstances" and the "compelling humanitarian considerations at stake".[180] This carefully worded ruling led the Court in *Bensaid v. the United Kingdom* to conclude that Article 3 would not be violated if the applicant were to be returned to Algeria, because although in a serious medical condition, medical treatment would be available for him in Algeria.[181] The Court thereby confirmed that it would exclude considerations that are purely humanitarian unless they found to be absolutely exceptional.

2. The second situation which may raise a problem under Article 3 of the ECHR is in cases of successive expulsion of an alien. The Commission recognised this situation very early on: in certain circumstances, the repeated expulsion of a foreigner without any identification and travel papers, and whose state of origin is unknown or refuses re-entry to its territory, may raise a problem with respect to Article 3.[182] The risk of successive expulsion has since become regulated, at least in Europe, by a series of readmission agreements, the Schengen Convention (now the protocol integrating the Schengen *acquis* into the framework of the European Union), and the Dublin Convention in cases of asylum seekers, in an attempt to reduce the phenomenon of "chain *refoulement*"[183] But the result remains unsatisfactory and the successive expulsion of aliens continues to raise concern under Article 3. This is particularly the case when it appears that in the process of removal the alien runs the risks of being sent to a third "unsafe" country. The definition of "safe country" was first discussed by the European Union ministers responsible for immigration matters in the Resolution on a Harmonised Approach to Questions concerning Host Third Countries (1992).[184] This concept has since become part of EU law following the adoption of the "Procedure Directive" in December 2005. It was agreed that all of the following requirements should be fulfilled for a third country to be considered as safe:

- the life and liberty of the returnee are not threatened in the third country on the basis of the grounds established in the 1951 Convention Relating to the Status of Refugees;

- the principle of *non-refoulement*, in accordance with the 1951 Convention Relating to the Status of Refugees, is respected;

- the prohibition of removal, in violation of the right to freedom from torture and cruel, inhuman or degrading treatment, is respected; and

- the possibility exists to request refugee status and, if found to be a refugee, to receive protection in accordance with the 1951 Convention Relating to the Status of Refugees.[185]

The Court pronounced on the issue of "chain *refoulement*" in *T.I. v. the United Kingdom*, and it extended the duty of non-expulsion under Article 3, read in conjunction with Article 1, to cases of "indirect removal ... to an intermediary country, which is also a Contracting State", thereby reminding European Union member states of their legal obligation to secure the protection of the rights guaranteed under the ECHR irrespective of their engagements under European Union/Community law.[186] The ruling of the Court in the *Bosphorus* case endorses this position and reaffirms that states remain responsible for all their discretionary actions, including those actions that are based on the law of the European Union/Community.[187]

3. The third situation is where an alien is subject to an expulsion order but is in no physical condition to travel. Quite early on, the Commission recognised that the expulsion of an alien whose life is in danger at the time of transportation, e.g., through hunger strike, could raise an issue under Article 2 or 3, irrespective of the applicant's voluntary self-infliction of the danger.[188]

4. The fourth situation concerns the manner in which an expulsion is carried out. Here the Court appears to interpret Article 3 restrictively. For instance, the Court found no violation of Article 3 in the case of a 9 year old being expelled with considerable haste and with all responsibility for her welfare being handed over to others as soon as she had left the territory.[189] Equally, in *Öcalan v. Turkey*, the Court found no violation of Article 3 when assessing the conditions in which the applicant had been transferred from Kenya to Turkey. In particular, the Court accepted the handcuffing and blindfolding of the applicant during his journey from Kenya to the Turkish prison as a necessary precaution to ensure smooth travel (e.g., to prevent him from absconding or causing injury to himself).[190]

In this context, it may be noted that the principles developed by the European Committee for the Prevention of Torture and Inhuman or Degrading Treatment or Punishment (hereinafter the CPT)[191] and the Court in the context of detention or police custody are directly relevant. Article 3, in particular, has been relied on successfully in several cases of ill-treatment of aliens in police custody pending deportation or "for the purpose of bringing him before the competent legal authority on reasonable suspicion of having committed an offence or when it is reasonably considered necessary to prevent his committing an offence or fleeing after having done so".[192]

The Court summarised the requirements of Article 3, in *Kalashnikov v. Russia*, as follows:

> the state must ensure that a person is detained in conditions which are compatible with respect for his human dignity; that the manner and method of the execution of the measure do not subject him to distress or hardship of an intensity exceeding the unavoidable level of suffering inherent in detention and that, given the practical demands of imprisonment, his health and well-being are adequately secured.[193]

It follows that anyone deprived of their liberty must be treated with dignity; it is no longer required to show the authorities' positive intention to humiliate or debase the victim.[194] This case law is being influenced more and more by the findings of the CPT.[195] For instance, the Court has recognised that "all forms of solitary confinement without appropriate mental and physical stimulation are likely, in the long-term, to have damaging effects, resulting in deterioration of mental faculties and social abilities".[196] However, in *Öcalan v. Turkey*, a case involving "the most dangerous terrorist in the country", the Court accepted that "extraordinary security measures" of detention be put in place, such as no access to television programmes or a telephone.[197] In *Ribitsch v. Austria*, a case of police custody, the Court recognised that any recourse to force should be made "strictly necessary", failing which the treatment would be found to diminish human dignity and violate Article 3.[198] Thus, any unnecessary and disproportionate recourse to force (e.g., beating and kicking, mouth- and nose-taping, or drug administering) by the police and immigration officers during the execution of an expulsion or extradition order could constitute a violation of Article 3. In *Price v. the United Kingdom*, the Court found a violation of Article 3 in the case of a disabled person whose prison cell was not adapted to her disability needs, i.e., too cold, the bed was too high, and the sink and toilet were inaccessible.[199] And in *Mouisel v. France*, the Court found that the serious illness of a detainee to be incompatible with continued detention; necessary medical assistance must indeed be available in the context of protection of the physical integrity of persons deprived of their liberty under Article 3.[200] The (old) age of a detainee may also be a relevant factor for the Court.[201] It follows that a minimum level of hygiene and adequate medical treatment must also be respected during the execution of an expulsion or extradition order.

Protection against ill-treatment during detention under Article 3 of the ECHR is further supplemented by the European Convention for the Prevention of Torture and Inhuman and Degrading Treatment or Punishment 1987.[202] This instrument establishes a system of prevention whereby an independent committee of experts is allowed to visit public places of detention (e.g., police stations, prison, detention centres, transit zones of airports) and to report on the conditions and treatment during detention "with a view to strengthening ... the protection of such persons from torture and from inhuman or degrading treatment or punishment".[203] The two systems of protection are nevertheless separate, and a negative finding by the committee under the CPT does not necessarily result in a finding of violation by the Court under Article 3 of the ECHR.[204]

In all cases of expulsion under Article 3 (or 2) there is a crucial element of urgency. Interim measures of protection can be indicated under the Rules of Procedure of the Court (Rule 39).[205] The rule is clearly designed to deal with emergency situations. Interim measures may only be granted by (a committee of) the Court (previously the Commission) in cases where an alien can show that "irreparable" or "irretrievable" damage would occur if s/he were expelled prior to a decision being taken on his/her case. The "irreparable" or "irretrievable" character of the damage is difficult to prove because the Court requires a certain degree of probability (i.e., factual or material evidence) that the applicant will risk being subjected to ill-treatment if returned to his or her country of origin before a decision is taken on the case.[206] Applications for interim measures have a suspensive effect in all cases of expulsion but, largely because of the non-binding character of interim measures, this effect was at the mercy of states' good will.[207] In February 2005, the Court's Grand Chamber nonetheless declared interim measures to be legally binding and held that the refusal by a contracting party to comply with an interim measure would constitute a violation of Article 34 of the ECHR.[208]

Cases of expulsion also raise the question of "just satisfaction to the injured party" under Article 41 of the ECHR. The Court's case law reveals that this is normally granted by the Court in the form of the judgment finding that the state would be responsible for a violation of Article 3 if it were to expel the alien and/or that the state is responsible for a wrongful application of the procedural safeguards embraced in the notion of positive obligation under Article 3. States have complied with these judgments in very different terms. In the United Kingdom, for instance, compliance has generally resulted in the withdrawal of the expulsion order and in the alien being authorised to remain on ECHR grounds and granted Humanitarian Protection (the "old" Exceptional Leave to Remain).[209] In Austria, however, aliens allowed to remain following the withdrawal of an expulsion order on the basis of Article 3 have been refused residence permits and denied the right to work.[210] Regrettably, the Court has so far been reluctant to extend the grounds for awards of "just satisfaction" under Article 41 to include minimum social protection.[211] Thankfully, most cases never reach the final stage of judgment by the Court and are struck off because governments agree to withdraw the expulsion order and to grant some sort of status to the applicant.[212] It may also be noted that within the European Union, the adoption of the "Qualification Directive" in April 2004 means that in 24 of the 25 member states of the European Union (Denmark having opted out of the application of this directive) persons allowed to stay on ECHR grounds shall be granted a status, albeit with lesser rights than refugees, but nonetheless a legal status.[213]

Basic means of subsistence under Articles 2 and 3

Article 2 may also be relevant concerning access to the basic means of subsistence of "everyone", including aliens, in the country of residence; but such cases have so far received lukewarm support from the Strasbourg organs. For instance, the Court declared inadmissible an application against Italy introduced by a national from Iraq who had been severely injured by a mine (while on a clearing mission), which had been manufactured and sold by Italy to Iraq.[214] However, in *Osman v. the United Kingdom,* admittedly not an immigration case, the Court accepted that there could be a breach of Article 2 even where the state was not guilty of gross negligence or intentional disregard to the duty to protect life.[215] Under this principle, it is not excluded that a state could become liable under Article 2 of the ECHR if it deprived an individual from his basic rights of subsistence. Such a broad interpretation is already accepted in countries such as the United Kingdom, where the House of Lords, in a landmark decision on the state's obligations towards destitute people, found that the Secretary of State for the Home Office's practice of refusing accommodation or food to those asylum seekers who fail to claim asylum promptly on arrival in the country is inhuman and degrading and as such constitutes a breach of Article 3 of the ECHR.[216] And in *Pancenko v. Latvia,* the Court held that "the Convention does not guarantee, as such, socio-economic rights, including the right to charge-free dwelling, the right to work, the right to medical assistance, or the right to claim financial assistance form a State to maintain a certain level of living". But quite importantly the Court recognised that living conditions could raise an issue under Article 3 if they attained a minimum level of severity.[217] Thus, as things stand, states remain free under the ECHR to deny a residence permit or the right to work or a minimum social protection to aliens allowed to remain on their territory. However, as previously indicated, both Articles 3 and 5 require that a minimum standard of treatment be respected for aliens in police custody. Furthermore, as will be discussed in the remainder of this section, other provisions of the ECHR, in particular Articles 6, 8, 13 and 14, provide certain standards in the treatment of aliens allowed to remain in a member state on the basis of Article 3.

Refusal of entry of a discriminatory character under Article 3

Discrimination may, under certain circumstances, be so serious that it constitutes in itself (and without reference to Article 14) degrading treatment contrary to Article 3. The principle was held in the context of refusal of entry of citizens of a state in the *East African Asians* cases where the Commission found that racial discrimination "could, in certain circumstances, in itself amount to degrading treatment within the meaning of Article 3".[218] The degree of severity of the treatment in this case was found to result from the combined effect of factors, including the fact that the applicants' continued residence in Africa became illegal and that being United Kingdom citizens they had nowhere else to go should the United Kingdom refuse them entry. This ruling was confirmed in *Abulaziz, Cabales and Balkandali v. the United Kingdom,* though the Court introduced a further requirement of intent to be shown for discrimination to amount to a violation of Article 3.[219] In spite of the Commission's emphasis in the *East African Asians* cases on "the special circumstances" surrounding the case, Harris et al. refute the idea that "more ordinary cases of racial discrimination would not be degrading in breach of Article 3".[220] They further argue that discrimination on other grounds than race may also be degrading in breach of Article 3 on the ground that Article 14 has offered special protection against such discrimination.[221] In a similar line of arguments, the Commission recognised the applicability of Article 3 (albeit in conjunction with Article 14) in the case of Gypsies whose nationality may be uncertain and are therefore refused identity papers and forced to leave a territory for failing to present any personal document.[222]

Non-respect of a procedural requirement

The Court has also recognised that the non-respect of a procedural element of Article 3 per se may result in a violation of Article 3.[223] In *Selmouni v. France,* for instance, the Court confirmed its case law that Article 3 entails both a negative and positive obligation on the part of states. It then went on to recognise (on the basis of the fundamental character of Article 3 read together with Article 1 of the ECHR) that "positive obligation" means that the state which is accused of violating Article 3 (or any other article such as Article 2 or 5) must proceed immediately to an official and effective investigation aiming at identifying and punishing the offenders and that the applicant must have access to this procedure of investigation.[224] This would be the case whether the allegation under Article 3 concerns ill-treatment in a purely domestic setting (e.g., during detention or police custody) or in an extraterritorial setting (e.g., expulsion), although there has not yet been a case on the latter situation. The implied duty of a state to investigate allegations of serious ill-treatment by a state agent was fully articulated by the Court in *Assenov and Others v. Bulgaria.*[225] In this case, the Court recalled its principle that "where an individual alleges to have been injured by ill-treatment in custody, the Government are under an obligation to provide a complete and sufficient explanation as to how the injuries were caused".[226] In particular, the state in question is under a positive obligation to conduct an effective official investigation that should lead to the identification and punishment of the persons responsible for the alleged violation. And in *M.C. v. Bulgaria,* the Court extended the duty of states to provide a thorough investigation in cases of alleged violation by private individuals. It follows that the non-respect of a procedure specific to Article 3 (or Article 2) can result in a violation of Article 3 (or 2) in just the same way as the non-respect of the substantive obligation would. This jurisprudence confirms the possibility of "double violation" of a provision of the ECHR, in this case

Article 3.[227] It follows that the procedural guarantees inherent in Article 3 (or 2) have the effect of reinforcing the right to an effective remedy under Article 13 of the ECHR.[228] As will be seen in the paragraph below, there is some substantive overlap between the implied state's duty of investigation under Article 3 and that under Article 13. The Grand Chamber in *Ilhan v. Turkey* indicated that, as a rule, Article 13 should constitute the appropriate legal basis for examining the lack of an effective investigation into an arguable claim based on Article 3.[229] In spite of this ruling, sections of the Court have continued to consider complaints concerning a lack of effective investigation under Article 3.[230]

Right to an effective remedy

Considering that expulsion and extradition procedures remain outside the ambit of Article 6 of the ECHR and that Article 1 of Protocol No. 7 is limited to aliens lawfully resident in the territory of a contracting state, Article 13 of the ECHR has proved to be a key provision in terms of guaranteeing certain procedural safeguards to aliens.[231] Article 13 provides that "Everyone whose rights and freedoms as set forth in this Convention are violated shall have an effective remedy before a national authority". Thus, Article 13 provides a more general obligation on states to provide an effective remedy than Article 6, and the Court, when faced with the choice, often chooses to consider the complaint under Article 13.[232] The rationale for Article 13 is to secure, at the national level, a remedy to enforce the substance of the rights and freedoms guaranteed in the ECHR, in whatever form that remedy takes in the domestic legal order.[233] Aliens do not have the right to an effective remedy against any decision concerning entry, settlement or expulsion because the ECHR does not guarantee such a right (to enter, to settle or to be free from expulsion). Thus, an alien may only claim a right to an effective remedy under national law against a decision refusing entry or settlement or a decision on expulsion if this decision allegedly violates a Convention right, such as Article 2, 3 or 8, and both claims must be brought together.[234] Article 13 does not require the finding of an actual violation by the national authority prior to a remedy becoming effective. This way, even if at the end of the procedure the Court finds no violation of the ECHR, the defendant state was nevertheless obliged to provide an effective remedy for the examination of the alleged violation.[235] According to the Court, Article 13 does not require a remedy in domestic law in respect of any supposed claim under the ECHR by an individual; the claim needs to be "arguable" (*défendable*).[236] The Court considers the notions of "arguability" (Article 13) and "manifestly ill-founded" (Article 35 (3)) to be conceptually different; however, it applies the same threshold in regard to both notions.[237] It follows from this interpretation that an alien would only have a right to an effective remedy against a decision of expulsion if his/her claim of an alleged violation of the ECHR is arguable, i.e., is found to be manifestly well-founded by a national authority.

According to the Court, for a remedy to be effective in the domestic legal order, it must meet three standards.[238]

- First, it must exist institutionally.[239] The national authority does not need to be a judicial authority, but if it is not (for example, if it is an Ombudsman), its powers and procedural guarantees are relevant in determining whether the remedy before it is effective. The key element for the Court is the capacity of the authority to provide an effective remedy in practice and in law. It may in this regard have to conduct a thorough and effective investigation. Thus, in *Aydin v. Turkey*, a case of alleged rape and ill-treatment of a female detainee and failure of authorities to conduct an effective investigation into her complaint that she was tortured in this way, the Court held that "the requirement of a thorough and effective investigation into an allegation of rape in custody at the hands of a state official ... implies that the victim be examined, with all appropriate sensitivity, by medical professionals with particular experience in this area and whose independence is not circumscribed by instructions given by the prosecuting authority as to the scope of the examination".[240]

- Second, for a remedy to be effective, it must be adequate, i.e., the remedy must be organised in such a way as to allow the competent national authority to deal with the substance of the complaint and to grant appropriate relief. However, the particular form of remedy is left to the discretion of states to decide. The Court has nevertheless set specific guidelines. In the context of Article 3, adequate remedy means that the national authority must be able to assess the element of risk primarily with reference to those facts which were known or ought to have been known to the state at the time of expulsion. Thus, in *Chahal v. the United Kingdom*, a case of deportation to India of six Sikh separatists for national security reasons, the Court held that "Given the irreversible nature of the harm that might occur if the risk of ill-treatment materialised and the importance the Court attaches to Article 3, the notion of an effective remedy under Article 13 requires independent scrutiny of the claim that there exist substantial grounds for fearing a real risk of treatment contrary to Article 3. This scrutiny must be carried out without regard to what the person may have done to warrant expulsion or to any perceived threat to the national security of the expelling state".[241] The Court found no such guarantees in the case of *Chahal*, and concluded "on the contrary, the Court's approach was one of satisfying themselves that the Home Secretary had balanced the risk to Mr Chahal against the danger to national security".[242] In *Jabari v. Turkey*, a case of risk of persecution if returned to Iran, the Court found that "the automatic and mechanical application of a short time-limit [five days] for submitting an asylum application" may be at variance with Article 3.[243] It then found a violation of Article 13, in conjunction with Article 3, on the ground that no assessment had been made by the national authorities of the applicant's claim to be at risk of returned to Iran.[243]

> • Third, for a remedy to be effective, it must be available to the individual. In the context of a claim against expulsion under Article 13 in conjunction with Article 3, this means two things: the rejected asylum seeker must have access to the appeal procedure, i.e., s/he must be in a position to initiate such appeal as a party,[245] and the appeal must have a suspensive effect.[246] For instance, in *Čonka v. Belgium,* a case of collective expulsion of Slovakian nationals, the Court considered that the domestic remedies theoretically available to the applicants could not reasonably have been accessed by them prior to their expulsion. And it found a violation of Article 13 in conjunction with Article 4 of Protocol No. 4.[247]

In accordance with the general principle of good faith, these principles constitute guarantees that member states must at all cost refer to when applying their own procedural rules, whether by way of incorporation in domestic legislation or by way of application in national practice.

In sum, as far as protection against expulsion is concerned, the Court refuses to pay any attention to the "person"; nationality and conduct of the applicant are clearly irrelevant factors to a determination of a violation of Article 2 or 3 under the ECHR.[248] Assessment of the treatment feared by the applicant alone is relevant to the Court and it applies the same principles settled some fifteen years ago to the different facts of each case. The ECHR has become a key instrument of protection against expulsion. However, the Court is reluctant to extend the scope of protection under Article 3 (or 2) to include the entitlement to a legal status, including minimum subsistence rights. As a result, the integration of aliens into the member states of the Council of Europe remains almost entirely at the discretion of states. As stated by Blake, not only is there a need for a legal status but also the ECHR has the capability to develop such a status.[249]

Qualified rights

Qualified rights are rights which may be restricted by the operation of other rights or by the needs of society. The qualifications to rights can be explained as follows:[250]

- Any restriction on the right must be prescribed by law.

- The restriction must be justified by one of the aims explicitly recognised in the ECHR.

- The restriction must be proved to be "necessary in a democratic society", i.e., it must fulfil a pressing social need, pursue a legitimate aim, and there must be a reasonable relationship of proportionality between the means employed and the aim pursued.

- In addition, the restriction must comply with the non-discriminatory clause.

The most common qualified rights under the ECHR are the right to respect for private and family life (Article 8), freedom of thought, conscience and religion (Article 9), freedom of expression (Article 10), and freedom of assembly and association (Article 11). Other qualified rights also include the right to marry (Article 12), the right to education (Article 2 of Protocol No. 1) and the right to freedom of movement (Article 2 of Protocol No. 4). Of these rights, Article 8 has shown itself by far to be the most relevant to aliens.

Private and family life under Article 8

Article 8 of the ECHR guarantees the right to respect for everyone's private and family life.[251] The Commission and the Court originally recognised the relevance and applicability of Article 8 of the ECHR to aliens seeking entry into the territory of a contracting state in order to join their respective wives lawfully residing there.[252] This principle was extended to cases of minors seeking entry into the territory of a contracting state in order to join their parents.[253] The Court relied for the first time on Article 8 in a case of deportation in *Berrehab v. the Netherlands*, where such deportation would lead to an unjustified interference with the right of family life in the country of residence.[254] This was confirmed in several other instances, such as *Moustaquim v. Belgium*.[255] Finally, the Court even recognised the application of Article 8 to cases specific to France, i.e., permanent exclusion from the French territory.[256] Thus, Article 8 imposes serious limitations on the scope of a contracting state's power of removal or of refusal of entry of an alien. Considering the sensitivity of the matter, the Court recognised that such limitations did not, however, "impose on a State a general obligation to respect the choice by married couples of the country of their matrimonial residence and to authorise family reunion in its territory".[257]

The principles applied by the Court in assessing the scope of states' obligations under Article 8 were summarised in *Gül v. Switzerland* as follows:

> The Court reiterates that the essential object of Article 8 is to protect the individual against arbitrary action by the public authorities. There may in addition be positive obligations inherent in effective "respect" for family life. However, the boundaries between the State's positive and negative obligations under this provision do not lend themselves to precise definition. The applicable principles are, none the less, similar. In both contexts regard must be had to the fair balance that has to be struck between the competing interests of the individual and of the community as a whole; and in both contexts the State enjoys a certain margin of appreciation.
>
> The present case concerns not only family life but also immigration, and the extent of a State's obligation to admit to its territory relatives of settled immigrants will vary according to the particular circumstances of the persons involved and the general interest. As a matter of well-established international law and subject to its treaty obligations, a State has the right to control the entry of non-nationals into its territory.

> Moreover, where immigration is concerned, Article 8 cannot be considered to impose on a State a general obligation to respect the choice of married couples of the country of their matrimonial residence and to authorise family reunion in its territory. In order to establish the scope of the State's obligations, the facts of the case must be considered.[258]

Beyond the scope of these principles, specific criteria in the application of Article 8 are lacking.[259] The Court follows a case-by-case approach, and a survey of the case law reveals consistency in its approach. In each case before it, the Court first establishes the existence of an interference with the right to respect for private and family life under Article 8 (1), prior to considering whether the interference can be justified under Article 8 (2), keeping in mind the wide margin of appreciation enjoyed by states in complying with the ECHR.

Although Article 8 protects both private and family life, for many years the Court's approach has been to rule exclusively on the basis of family life within the context of Article 8 (1), while implicitly referring to elements of private life when considering the requirement of "necessary in a democratic society" under Article 8 (2).[260] In this regard, it has been willing to interpret the concept of family quite widely.[261] The Court has so far explicitly recognised the existence of family life between members of the nuclear family, that is, spouses, and parents and their minor children.[262] It seems also to have implicitly recognised family life from ties between near relatives in the context of the family reunion of an alien.[263] *Chorfi v. Belgium* offers the first instance in which the Court decided to consider the relevance of Article 8 (1) in the light of private and family life. There, it recognised that "private life … encompasses the right for an individual to form and develop relationships with other human beings, including relationships of a professional or business nature".[264] And in *Slivenko v. Latvia* even recognised the relevance of Article 8 (1) to displaced persons in the light of private life taken alone.[265]

It is clear for the Court that the "essential object of Article 8 is to protect the individual against arbitrary action by the public authorities", that is, the state must not interfere with the enjoyment of the right to private and family life; states are nevertheless left with a wide margin of appreciation.[266] For the Court, refusal to enter into (or removal from) the territory of a contracting state in order to be reunited with a family member or removal from the territory of a contracting state leading to the break-up of family life may only constitute "interference" if three requirements are met. First, there must be an effective family life. Second, the state against which the proceedings have been brought must in fact be the author of the violation.[267] Third, obstacles must exist against continuing a normal family life elsewhere, including the alien's country of origin. The Court's approach to the question whether it is reasonable to expect aliens to develop normal family life elsewhere is particularly restrictive towards aliens seeking entry for the purpose of family creation, i.e., the members of the family have never lived together or have lived apart for a very long time. The Court systematically affirms the principle that Article 8 cannot be held to impose on states a duty to respect immigrants' choice of residence and to authorise family reunion on their territory. It then proceeds to balance the applicant's right to family life against the state's right to control immigration at the early stage of establishing interference. As a result, no interference has yet been found by the Court.[268] The Court has adopted a more liberal approach towards aliens already present in the territory of a member state. It usually recognises the act of expulsion, deportation or permanent exclusion of a territory per se to constitute an interference, provided the act is certain and enforceable.[269] And, in contrast with cases of entry, the Court will usually balance the individual's rights against the community's interest after a lack of respect for the right to private and family life has been found, that is to say only when considering whether the interference is "necessary in a democratic society" in the light of Article 8 (2).[270]

It is regrettable that the Court failed to provide adequate reasons for distinguishing between cases of entry and cases of removal of aliens, for such distinction seems difficult to reconcile in practice. Any refusal to admit a family member, particularly a child, to the territory of a member state, indeed, suggests a strong expectation that the person lawfully residing in the territory will have to return to his/her country of origin. It thus seems extraordinary that the Court chose to differentiate these cases.[271] It follows that in cases of entry, interference will be established only if the individual shows that the state has overstepped its wide margin of appreciation. This makes proof difficult to establish in cases where the family does not even live together, and the individual seeking leave to enter has more links with the country of origin than with the country in which the rest of the family resides. The burden of proof is less stringent in cases of removal. This is because the individual is already living with his/her family in the country in question. Thus interference will not be difficult to establish. It is only in these cases that the Court will give careful consideration to all factors connecting the individual to the state of residence against the "pressing social need".

According to Article 8 (2), the right to respect for private and family life is not unlimited. Interference by a public authority with the exercise of the right to respect for private and family life may indeed be justified if it is "in accordance with the law", motivated by one or more of the legitimate aims listed, and "necessary in a democratic society", i.e., it is proportionate to the legitimate aim pursued. For a measure to be "in accordance with the law", it must have a basis in domestic law, be accessible and be foreseeable, i.e., "it must not be deprived of all guarantees against arbitrariness".[272] The requirement that the interfering measure be "necessary in a democratic society" necessitates the Court to balance the individual's rights against the community's interests while at the same time keeping in mind the wide margin of appreciation afforded to national authorities in the field of immigration. In cases of aliens seeking not to be removed because this would result in separating them from family members in the country or giving up an established private life, the Court requires the state to show that the interfering measure responds to a pressing social need, and in particular is proportionate to the legitimate aim pursued.[273] In its earlier cases, the Court considered that when serious offences have been committed by fully integrated aliens, or by aliens who have been resident for many years in the state in question, "other circumstances of the case relating to both applicants or to one of them only, are enough to compensate for this important fact".[274] And, the Court considers elements of family life but also private life, e.g., the length of the stay in question, to be particularly relevant. As a result, it has often found the interfering measure to be disproportionate in cases involving integrated aliens.[275] However, this approach has evolved in later cases. In particular, the length of the stay in the state in question alone is no longer considered a sufficient element to prevent removal.[276] Further factors combined with that element are necessary, such as, for instance, strong family ties and being born in the country in question.[277] Finally, the Court's case law also reveals strong support for states' firmness with regard to drug offences and other particularly grave offences.[278]

Thus, the Court continues to apply the principle established in the landmark cases, i.e., provided strong family links exist only exceptional circumstances can justify the removal of an integrated alien; a criminal sentence in the country of integration is generally regarded as sufficient.[279] The Court seems to prefer a subjective appreciation of the degree of separation experienced by the applicant to any specific criteria when balancing the individual's rights against the community's interests.[280] Its appreciation has developed from a focus on elements supporting integrated aliens' rights, such as length of stay, schooling, and social and business ties, to other elements. It seems now to give primary consideration to the existence of strong and effective family ties.[281] It is now also looking more closely at the seriousness of offences.[282] It seems, however, that although Article 8 protects "everyone" against interference by a public authority, the formal status of the applicant may be circumstantial in the finding by the Court of a violation of Article 8. Indeed, it follows from the Court's approach towards integrated aliens that persons recognised as refugees under the 1951 Convention Relating to the Status of Refugees and persons granted a residence permit on the ground of Article 3 of the ECHR would have no difficulty convincing the Court that a return to their (by definition unsafe) country of origin would either constitute a serious obstacle against establishing family life there, or be disproportionate to the protection of the community's interest. But this is often unnecessary. Once it has found a violation of Article 3 of the ECHR, the Court does not consider it necessary to investigate a complaint in the light of Article 8, and such cases have so far been decided on the basis of Article 3.[283] The Court has dealt with a complaint under Article 8, outside the scope of Article 3, in only two cases. Both were cases where the applicant was a beneficiary of subsidiary protection seeking entry of a young family member and the complaint was dismissed at the early stage of Article 8 (1), i.e., on the ground that no interference with the right to respect for private and family life existed.[284] The situation therefore remains uncertain in cases where the applicant is the beneficiary of a residence permit on grounds other than Article 3 ECHR.[285]

Finally, Article 8 may also be relevant to situations of expulsion in cases where the treatment in the country of return falls short of the Article 3 threshold. The landmark case on this issue is *Bensaid v. the United Kingdom*.[286] The applicant was suffering from a psychotic illness and he had been allowed to remain in the UK until given notice to leave the country. He submitted that his removal to Algeria would constitute a violation of Article 3 of the ECHR because he would not receive the degree of support and access to medical facilities which he currently relies on in the UK. The Court, relying on *D. v. the United Kingdom*, concluded that his expulsion to Algeria would not violate Article 3. The applicant further argued that his removal would have a severely damaging effect on his private life in the sense of his moral and physical integrity under Article 8. The Court did "not exclude that treatment which does not reach the severity of Article 3 treatment may nonetheless breach Article 8 in its private life aspect where there are sufficiently adverse effects on physical and moral integrity".[287] The Court went on to explain that private life covers the physical and psychological integrity of a person. It protects a "right to identity and personal development, and the right to establish and develop relationships with other human beings and the outside world".[288] Private life includes elements such as gender, identification, name, sexual orientation and sexual life. Mental health must also be regarded as a crucial part of private life associated with the aspect of moral integrity. However, the Court found that the applicant had not sufficiently established that he would suffer inhuman and degrading treatment or be affected to a degree falling within the scope of Article 8 if he returned to Algeria. Thus, the approach of the Court in this judgment seems to rest on a strong interdependent relationship in practice between Article 3 and Article 8. It follows that in cases where the illness of an applicant and the conditions in the country of return lead to a finding of a violation of Article 3, there is no need to consider Article 8.[289] Of more unfortunate consequences for aliens is the Court's recognition that in cases where the risk of alleged ill-treatment in the country of return is found not to be real enough to meet the threshold of Article 3, the applicant will also fail for the same reason under Article 8. Thus, whether under Article 3 or Article 8, expulsion cannot be objected to simply on the grounds that medical treatment or facilities are better or more accessible in the country ordering the expulsion than in the country to which the applicant is to be expelled. Clearly, the Court is reluctant to recognise a general human right to good physical and mental health in cases of expulsion.[290] The reason for this may be that in such cases the direct responsibility of the Contracting State for the infliction is never of concern.

Freedom of thought, conscience and religion, freedom of expression and freedom of assembly and association under Articles 9 to 11

Articles 9 to 11 may also raise particular issues for aliens in cases of expulsion but there is little case law to illustrate this. Just as in the case of other rights and freedoms guaranteed under the ECHR, the Commission has confirmed that Articles 9 to 11 do not grant aliens a right of settlement in a member state of the Council of Europe; thus expulsion does not constitute an interference with the freedoms guaranteed under Articles 9 to 11.[291] However, the refusal of entry or the expulsion of aliens may violate Articles 9 to 11 of the ECHR if they are aimed at restricting the exercise of their right to freedom of thoughts, conscience, religion, expression, assembly or association. Under paragraph 2 of Articles 9 to 11, states are nevertheless recognised as possessing the power to limit such freedoms in ways that "are prescribed by law and are necessary in a democratic society in the interests of public safety, for the protection of public order, health or morals, or for the protection of the rights and freedoms of others". In addition, Article 16 allows states to impose restrictions on the political rights of aliens, notwithstanding the freedom guaranteed in Articles 10 and 11.[292] Thus, "the prohibition of political demonstrations by migrant workers in the host state against the Government of their country of origin might be justified on the basis of Article 16 'if in the interest of good relations with other states'".[293] The case *Piermont v. France*, nonetheless, shows that the Court is willing to interpret the concept of "aliens" narrowly. In particular, it rejected the application of Article 16 to a national of a member state of the European Union (i.e., Germany) and an MEP, thereby finding that the expulsion measure constituted an interference which was unjustified under Articles 56, 16 or 10 (2). It concluded therefore that since the measure of expulsion "was not necessary in a democratic society, there has been a breach of Article 10".[294] More recently, in a non-expulsion context, the Court found a violation of both Articles 9 and 10. The Court, in particular, found a violation of Article 9 on the ground that "the restrictions placed on the freedom of movement ... considerably curtailed [the applicants'] ability to observe their religious beliefs, in particular, their access to places of worship outside their villages and their participation in other aspects of religious life".[295] The Court also found a violation of Article 10 in respect of Greek Cypriots living in northern Cyprus "in so far as school-books destined for use in their primary school were subject, during the period under consideration, to excessive measures of censorship".[296] The Court did not, however, find, beyond reasonable doubt, that "an administrative practice of violating the right of the enclaved Greek Cypriots to freedom of association [under Article 11] existed".[296] It follows that Articles 9 to 11 are of rather limited use to aliens in the context of entry or expulsion.

The right to marry under Article 12

Closely related to the notion of family life in Article 8 is the right to marry and to found a family under Article 12 of the ECHR. Unlike Article 8, Article 12 has been interpreted strictly by the Strasbourg organs and has proved to be of limited application to aliens.[298] Although the Commission has sometimes considered the right to found a family as an "absolute right" in that the state may not indeed interfere with the right itself, the exercise of the right to marry is in fact subject to national laws. Hence, states are left with a wide margin of appreciation in the "exercise" of the right to marry and to found a family.[299] Thus, in the case of a Dutch couple who wanted to adopt a foreign child, the Commission recognised that adoption fell within the ambit of Article 12, thereby recognising that the conditions on the right to adopt imposed by national laws were subject to control by the Strasbourg organs.[300] However, having considered the conditions laid down in the Dutch Aliens Circular, i.e., only foreign children under school age could be fostered, and the difference in age between the foreign child and each of the potential parents should not exceed forty years, the Commission found that the Dutch authorities did not violate the right to found a family under Article 12 as regulated by Dutch law. In addition, it found the authorities not liable for any discriminatory treatment under Article 14 in conjunction with Article 12, since the difference of treatment (between the adoption of a foreign child and a Dutch child) had an objective basis and a legitimate purpose in the interest of foreign foster children (i.e., foreign foster children should receive their basic school education at the same age as Dutch children in order to facilitate their integration).

The right to education

The first sentence of Article 2 of Protocol No.1 provides: "No person shall be denied the right to education". The scope of this provision was recently summarised by the Grand Chamber in *Leyla Şahin v. Turkey*, a case in which the applicant, a student in medicine at Istanbul University, was refused permission to attend lectures or sit exams because she was wearing the Islamic headscarf. In this case, the Court considered the scope of the first sentence of Article 2 of Protocol No. 1 in light of previous case law, and confirmed that this provision did not require the state to create any particular type of education but rather that it recognised to everyone within the jurisdiction of a contracting state the right to avail themselves of the means of instruction existing at a given time.[301] It also re-emphasised that this right refers to all levels of education, i.e., nursery, primary, secondary, and higher education, including university. The Court then discussed the following general principles. First, the right not to be denied education includes "the right of access to educational institutions" as well as "the right to obtain ... official recognition of the studies which he has completed".[302] Second, in spite of its importance, this right is not absolute; it may indeed be subject to limitations.

This general principle was first held by the Court in the *Belgian Linguistic Case*:[303] this right "by its very nature calls for regulation by the State, regulation which may vary in time and place according to the needs and resources of the community and of individuals"[304] as well as to the "distinctive features of different levels of education".[305] Thus, the contracting parties enjoy a certain margin of appreciation and any restriction imposed on the right to education must be "foreseeable for those concerned and pursue a legitimate aim".[306] Furthermore, any limitation on the right to education must be proportionate to the aim sought to be achieved.[307] Finally, such restriction must not conflict with any other rights enshrined in the ECHR and its protocols. Note that in *Timishev v. Russia*, the Court conceded a narrow margin of appreciation by holding that the prohibition to "deny the right to education" contained in Article 2 of Protocol No. 1 had no stated exceptions and that "its structure is similar to that of Articles 2 and 3, Article 4 § 1 and Article 7 of the Convention ('No one shall ...'), which together enshrine the most fundamental values of the democratic societies making up the Council of Europe".[308] Thus, a restrictive interpretation of this prohibition would not be consistent with the aim or purpose of Article 1 of Protocol No. 2.[309] It follows from the above case law that aliens lawfully resident in a contracting state have the right of access to the existing education facilities. This right does not include "a right for parents to have education conducted in a language other than that of the country in question".[310] However, it does include the right of parents to ensure such education and teaching in conformity with their own religious and philosophical convictions.[311] It follows that "members of religious or philosophical minorities have the right to establish their own schools".[312] Read in connection with Article 14 of the ECHR, Article 2 of Protocol No. 1 would suggest that education should be available to nationals and aliens alike, including their children, unless there is an objective and reasonable justification for differential treatment.[313] This would be the case, in particular, in order to facilitate the integration of children of aliens into the society, as provided under international law.[314]

However, Article 2 of Protocol No. 1 does not go as far as to guarantee a right of entry into or establishment in a country in order to receive education there. In the case *15 Foreign Students v. the United Kingdom*, the Commission found that "Article 2, first sentence, does not grant a right for an alien to stay in a given country. An alien's 'right to education' is independent of his right, if any, to stay in the country and does not protect or, as a corollary, include this latter right. The refusal of permission to remain in the country cannot be regarded as an interference with the right to education, but only as a control of immigration which falls outside the scope of Article 2".[315] However, the Commission did not exclude the possibility that Article 2 might be at issue in a case where expulsion would result in the applicant being denied any elementary education in his/her country of destination.[316] Article 2 may not be interpreted as recognising a right of entry in a contracting state either.

In this respect, the Commission also rejected the interpretation that Article 2 may include the right to enter to teach.[317]

The right to leave a country under Article 2 (2) of Protocol No. 4

Article 2 of Protocol No. 4 provides for "Freedom of movement". The scope of paragraph 1 of this provision has already been discussed in the context of derogations against the principle of non-discrimination between nationals and aliens.[318] Here it is more the scope of paragraph 2 of Article 2 which calls for consideration. It provides that "Everyone shall be free to leave any country, including his own". As in the case of Articles 8 to 11, the rights guaranteed in paragraph 2 of Article 2 (but also paragraph 1) are subject to those restrictions which are "in accordance with the law" and are "necessary in a democratic society" on limited grounds. Also, as in the case of Articles 8 to 11, these restrictions are subject to the principle of proportionality and to the doctrine of the "margin of appreciation". Thus, the Court ruled, in the recent case *Riener v. Bulgaria*, that an applicant who owed a large amount of taxes could not, however, be restricted in her freedom of movement (i.e., in the form of a travel ban) for an indefinite period of time, and that such "restriction on the right to leave one's country on ground of unpaid debt could only be justified as long as it served its aim – recovering the debt".[319] In the past, the Commission has also expressed the view that the right to leave a state's territory does not impose a duty on the state to facilitate entry into any one country in particular.[320]

Limited rights

Limited rights are rights which may only be limited in very specific circumstances and ways, and unlike in the case of qualified rights, states have a lesser margin of discretion when securing these rights to everyone within their jurisdiction.

Right to a fair trial

Article 6 of the ECHR guarantees procedural rights, including the right to "a fair and public hearing within a reasonable time by an independent and impartial tribunal established by law" (paragraph 1). The provisions of this article apply, as indeed all other provisions of Section I of the ECHR, to "everyone" within the jurisdiction of a contracting party, i.e., nationals and aliens. It is nevertheless difficult for aliens to invoke successfully Article 6 (1) in respect of expulsion or refusal to grant a residence permit in a state, because the provisions of Article 6 only apply to certain proceedings.[321] As far as aliens are concerned these proceedings are of two types:

- Article 6 (1) may apply in cases where an applicant is being returned to a third country where s/he may be subjected to treatment contrary to Article 6 (1). The extraterritorial effect of Article 6 was recognised in *Soering v. the United Kingdom* concerning the extradition to the United States of Mr Soering, who was claiming that the absence of legal aid in the State of Virginia would prevent him from securing legal representation as required by Article 6.[322] The Court found that it "does not exclude that an issue might exceptionally be raised under Article 6 by an extradition decision in circumstances where the fugitive has suffered or risks suffering a flagrant denial of fair trial in the requesting country. However, the facts of the present case do not disclose such a risk".[323] This approach was confirmed in *Drozd and Janousek v. France and Spain,* where the Court stated that although states parties to the ECHR do not have to ensure that the guarantees of Article 6 will be respected in the receiving country, "the Contracting States are, however, obliged to refuse their co-operation [in the administration of justice] if it emerges that the conviction is the result of a flagrant denial of justice".[324] The same standard of "flagrant denial" was used by the Commission in a case of detention pending expulsion, *M.A.R. v. the United Kingdom.*[325] The applicant complained that his expulsion to Iran would constitute a violation of Articles 2, 3, 5 and 6. He had been granted refugee status in the United Kingdom, but following two successive convictions for drug-related offences, he was ordered to be deported to Iran. The applicant argued, in particular, that his drug convictions exposed him to the risk of being charged, tried and sentenced to death by the Islamic Revolutionary Court in an arbitrary way, i.e., to the risk of "flagrant denial of justice". The Commission declared the application admissible in respect of Article 6 on that ground, i.e., "flagrant denial of justice".

• Article 6 (1) may also apply in asylum and expulsion proceedings, but this interpretation has not yet been recognised by the Court. Indeed, for many years the Commission refused to recognise the application of Article 6 (1) to cases of entry, establishment and expulsion of aliens from the territory of a contracting state on the ground that its scope is restricted to "the determination of civil rights and obligations or … any criminal charge" and that immigration proceedings do not involve civil rights and obligations nor do they amount to a determination of a criminal charge.[326] It nevertheless reversed this well-established case law in its admissibility decision in *Maaouia v. France.*[327] This case involved a national from Tunisia sentenced to six years' imprisonment for armed robbery and armed assault with intent. Following his release, a deportation order was made against him. Unaware of the order, he refused to leave French territory and was sentenced to one year's imprisonment, following which an order of exclusion was made against him. The applicant complained that the length of the proceedings for the rescission of the exclusion order was unreasonable, and therefore in breach of Article 6 (1) of the ECHR. The Commission found the application admissible and, for the first time, decided to refer such a case to the Court. In a restrictive judgment, the Court simply confirmed the classical case law of the Commission that Article 6 (1) does not apply to such proceedings.[328] In particular, it found that the proceedings for the rescission of an exclusion order did not concern the determination of civil rights. It relied for this on the existence of Article 1 of Protocol No. 7, which contains procedural guarantees applicable in the expulsion of aliens (a protocol ratified by France) to exclude any such guarantee from Article 6 (1).[329] Furthermore, it considered that exclusion orders did not concern the determination of a criminal charge either, as confirmed by the criminal legal systems of the member states of the Council of Europe.[330] In their dissenting opinion, Judges Loucaides and Traja expressed the regret that "both the Court and the Commission have shown great reluctance to interpret in a liberal way the concept of 'civil rights and obligations'". In the absence of a definition of the word "civil" in the ECHR, they decided to refer to Article 31 (a) of the Vienna Convention on the Law of Treaties as tools for interpretation, and they suggested that, in the *context* of Article 6 (1), the word "civil" simply means "non-criminal". They pointed to the fact that the Court itself has been willing to extend the concept of "civil rights and obligations" to matters falling outside the strictly defined private law sphere, e.g., claims for social security and social assistance, judge's pension.[331] Thus, in the light of the object and purpose of the ECHR, Article 6 (1) should be given the broadest possible meaning; the principle of *good faith* supports this approach.

Conclusion

According to Article 1 of the ECHR, *everyone* within the jurisdiction of a contracting party benefits from the rights and freedoms enumerated therein. In theory, therefore, alienage constitutes no ground for discrimination under the ECHR. In reality, however, the classical divide between aliens and nationals has remained and aliens continue to be in a vulnerable position under the ECHR. This is particularly true concerning their political and residence rights. Thus, aliens are denied political rights irrespective of their length of residence in a country and certain other rights and freedoms of aliens may be limited on a number of grounds (e.g., family life, freedom of association). Safeguards against the expulsion of aliens are only procedural and may be overridden, even if they are lawfully present in a country. At the centre of this divide lies the absence of a generous and progressive concept of equality. Fundamental values of justice call for the inclusion of the experiences of aliens in the application of the law, including the ECHR. In this regard, Protocol No. 12 will play an important role by widening the scope of the non-discrimination clause to "any right set forth by law", not just those rights and freedoms protected under the ECHR. However, this protocol remains non-ratified by the majority of the contracting parties to the ECHR. In spite of this assessment, the mere fact that states agree to the ECHR limits their sovereignty with respect to the treatment of aliens. Restrictions on sovereignty are further manifested in the supervisory and enforcement mechanism of the ECHR.

Notes

1 In June 2006, Belarus and Montenegro remain the only candidates for membership still outside the Council of Europe.

2 As amended by Protocols Nos. 3, 5, 8 and 11, which entered into force on 21 September 1970, 20 December 1971, 1 January 1990 and 1 November 1998 respectively.

3 Protocol No. 1 (adopted in 1952, in force since 1954); Protocol No. 4 (adopted in 1963, in force since 1968) securing certain rights and freedoms other than those already included in the Convention and in Protocol No. 1 ; Protocol No. 6 concerning the abolition of the death penalty (adopted in 1983, in force since 1985); Protocol No. 7 (adopted in 1984, in force since 1988); and Protocol No. 13 concerning the abolition of the death penalty in all circumstances (adopted in 2002, in force since 2003).

4 Protocol No. 11 to the Convention for the Protection of Human Rights and Fundamental Freedoms, restructuring the control machinery established thereby (adopted in 1994, in force since 1 November 1998).

5 G. Goodwin-Gill, *International law and the movement of persons between states* (1978), 58-63. J. Hathaway, *The rights of refugees under international law* (2005), 75-83 and 147-153.

6 I. Brownlie, *Principles of public international law* (1998), 526-531. R. Cholewinski, *Migrant workers in international human rights law* (1997), 40-47. For a critical account of the duty of equal protection of non-citizens and the duty of non-discrimination in international human rights law, see J. Hathaway, op. cit., *supra* note 5, 123-147.

7 G. Goodwin-Gill, op. cit., *supra* note 5, 75-87.

8 R. Higgins, "The European Convention on Human Rights", in *Human rights in international law* (Theodor Meron, ed., 1984), 495-549, at 537.

9 For a traditional perspective on international law, see *Oppenheim's International Law*, Jennings & Watts eds. (9th ed, 1996), paragraphs 620, 376, 379.

10 (1978), paragraph 239. The full text of all the judgments and decisions of the Strabsourg institutions is available on HUDOC. This can be accessed through the website of the Council of Europe (www.coe.int) at http://cmiskp.echr.coe.int/tkp197/search.asp?skin=hudoc-en

11 [1970] ICJ Reports, 3.

12 *Loizidou v. Turkey*, (1995), paragraph 75. See also, G. Cohen-Jonathan, "L'affaire Loizidou devant la Cour européenne des Droits de l'Homme. Quelques observations", *Revue générale de droit international public* (1998), 123, and J. Andriantsimbazovina, "L'élaboration progressive d'un ordre public européen des droits de l'homme. Réflexions à propos de la jurisprudence de la Cour européenne des Droits de l'Homme de 1988 à 1995", *Cahiers de droit européen* 33 (1997), 670.

13 R. Higgins, *Problems and process, international law and how we use it* (1994), at 96.

14 In *D. v. the United Kingdom* (judgment of 2 May 1997, paragraph 48), the Court explained that even if the applicant never entered the United Kingdom in the technical sense, he had been within the jurisdiction, in custody, at Gatwick airport, and for the Court it was sufficient that "he had been physically present there".

15 R. Wallace, *Companion to the European Convention on Human Rights –
    Vol. I* (1999), at 4.

16 *Soering v. the United Kingdom*, judgment of 7 July 1989. See also, *Drozd
    and Janousek v. France and Spain* (judgment of 26 June 1992) in which
    the Court accepted the concept of "jurisdiction" under Article 1 ECHR
    to include situations where acts of the member states, whether
    performed within or outside national frontiers, produce effects outside
    their own territory (paragraphs. 91-97).

17 *Oppenheim's*, op. cit., *supra* note 9, paragraphs 626.

18 G. Goodwin-Gill, *The refugee in international law* (2nd edn 1996), 167-170.
    See also UNHCR's submission to the European Court of Human Rights in
    T.I. v. the United Kingdom, admissibility decision of 7 March 2000.

19 *Banković and Others v. Belgium and 16 Other Contracting States*, (in)ad-
    missibility decision of 12 December 2001, paragraphs 67 and 71.

20 Harris, O'Boyle and Warbrick, *Law of the European Convention on
    Human Rights* (1995), at 3. In this regard Article 53 ("Safeguard for
    existing human rights") provides "Nothing in this Convention shall be
    construed as limiting or derogating from any of the human rights and
    fundamental freedoms which may be ensured under the laws of any
    High Contracting Party or under any other agreement to which it is a
    Party."

21 As of 1 August 2006, Protocol No. 1 remains unsigned (and therefore
    also non-ratified) by Andorra, and signed but non-ratified by Monaco
    and Switzerland. Protocol No. 4 ("securing rights and freedoms other
    than those already included in the Convention and in the First Protocol
    thereto") remains unsigned by Andorra, Greece and Switzerland; in
    addition, it is still to be ratified by Spain, Turkey and the United
    Kingdom. Protocol No. 6 ("concerning the abolition of the death
    penalty") remains non-ratified by Russia. Protocol No. 7 remains
    unsigned by Andorra and the United Kingdom; it is still to be ratified
    by Belgium, Germany, the Netherlands, Spain and Turkey. Protocol
    No. 12 remains unsigned by Andorra, Bulgaria, Denmark, France,
    Lithuania, Malta, Monaco, Poland, Sweden, Switzerland and the United
    Kingdom. It is still to be ratified by 21 countries. Protocol No. 13
    remains unsigned by Azerbaijan and Russia; it is still to be ratified by
    Albania, Armenia, France, Italy, Latvia, Moldova, Poland and Spain.

22 See also Article 17 prohibiting any abuse of the rights and freedoms
    guaranteed in the ECHR. Thus, any limitation of a right or freedom
    guaranteed under the ECHR must be strictly interpreted within the
    extent that is provided in the ECHR.

23 Following the events of 9/11, the United Kingdom introduced anti-
    terrorist legislation aiming at the indefinite detention of terrorist
    suspects and a derogation order relating to Article 5 (1) *f* of the ECHR.
    Both measures were challenged successfully before the House of Lords
    on the grounds of being disproportionate and that the "decision to
    detain one group of suspected international terrorists, defined by
    nationality or immigration status, and not another" was contrary to
    Article 14 of the ECHR (as per Lord Bingham of Cornhill, paragraphs 68).
    The House of Lords in particular referred to long established case law
    by the European Court of Human Rights on "public emergency", e.g.,
    Lawless v. Ireland (No. 3) (1961), *Greek case* (1969), and *Ireland v. the United*

Kingdom (1978). See, *A (FC) and others (FC) v. Secretary of State for the Home Department*, House of Lords, judgment of 16 December 2004.

24 S. Livingstone, "Article 14 and the prevention of discrimination in the ECHR", *European Human Rights Reports* (1997), at 33. He refers to the case of *Lindsay v. the United Kingdom*, in which the Commission recognised a measure of positive discrimination (in the area of taxation policy) as being justified to encourage married women into the labour market.

25 *Handyside v. the United Kingdom* (judgment of 7 December 1976, para. 48) and *Aksoy v. Turkey* (judgment of 18 December 1996, paragraph 51). Cf. also Articles 1 (obligation to secure human rights), 13 (right to an effective remedy) and 35 (1) (exhaustion of domestic remedies) but also Articles 38 and 39 (friendly settlement).

26 M. Shaw, *International law* (5th edn, 2003), at 323. *Tyrer v. the United Kingdom*, judgment of 25 April 1978, paragraphs 31. The Court has also underlined the decisive role of the object and purpose when interpreting the provisions of the ECHR (see, e.g., *König v. the Federal Republic of Germany*, judgment of 28 June 1978, para. 88). For an excellent (critical) assessment of the use by the Court of the principles of interpretation, see O. de Schutter, "L'interprétation de la Convention européenne des Droits de l'Homme: un essai en démolition", *Revue de droit international et de sciences diplomatiques et politiques*, 70 (1992), 83-127.

27 *Selmouni v. France*, judgment of 28 July 1999, paragraph 101.

28 Ibid., paragraph 80. Through this finding, the Court was re-emphasising the fact that priority ought to be given to effective protection over excessive formalism (paragraph 77).

29 G. Cohen-Jonathan, "Un arrêt de principe de la «nouvelle» Cour européenne des Droits de l'Homme: *Selmouni v. France* (28 juillet 1999)", *Revue générale de droit international public* 2000-1, 181, at 192.

30 A. Drzemczewski, "A major overhaul of the European human rights Convention control mechanism: Protocol No. 11", *Collected courses of the Academy of European Law – Recueil des cours de l'Académie de droit européen*, 1995, Volume VI, Book 2 (1997), 121-210.

31 Steiner and Alston, *International human rights in context* (2000), at 804. See, more recently, *Cyprus v. Turkey*, judgment of 10 May 2001.

32 Article 46 ECHR.

33 P. Mahoney, "Speculating on the future of the reformed European Court of Human Rights", *Human Rights Law Journal* 20 (2000), 1-4.

34 Explanatory report to Protocol No. 14 to the Convention for the Protection of Human Rights and Fundamental Freedoms, amending the control system of the Convention, available at: http://conventions.coe.int/Treaty/EN/Reports/Html/194.htm

35 Shearer, *Starke's international law* (1994), at 314. R. Plender, *International migration law* (1988), at 1. L. Henkin, "An agenda for the next century: the myth and mantra of state sovereignty", *Virginia Journal of International Law* (1994), 115-120.

36 R. Plender, op. cit., *supra* note 35, at 1. *Oppenheim's*, op. cit., *supra* note 9, paragraph 400.

37 EC Treaty, as amended by the Amsterdam Treaty, 1997, Articles 18, 19, 39, 40 and 43.

38 EC Treaty, as amended by the Amsterdam Treaty, Title IV.

39 See generally, C. Beyani, *Human rights standards and the movement of people within states* (2000).

40 "1. Everyone lawfully within the territory of a State shall, within that territory, have the right to liberty of movement and freedom to choose his residence.

2. Everyone shall be free to leave any country, including his own.

3. No restrictions shall be placed on the exercise of these rights other than such as are in accordance with law and are necessary in a democratic society in the interests of national security or public safety, for the maintenance of *ordre public,* for the prevention of crime, for the protection of health or morals, or for the protection of rights and freedoms of others.

4. The rights set forth in paragraph 1 may also be subject, in particular, areas, to restrictions imposed in accordance with law and justified by the public interest in a democratic society".

41 Goodwin-Gill, op. cit., *supra* note 5, 147-159.

42 This power includes the right to expel, deport or extradite aliens; it does not extend to one's own nationals (e.g., Article 3 of Protocol No. 4 to the ECHR). See generally, *Oppenheim's,* op. cit., *supra* note 9, 940-948. See also, Swiss Delegation of the CAHAR, "Obligations incumbent on states under public international law with respect to the readmission of their own nationals and aliens", Council of Europe, CAHAR (96) 12 (1996), 3-44.

43 This duty is often regulated in the form of bilateral or multilateral readmission agreements. In the case of refugees, it is suggested that this duty ceases "until such time as the refugee willingly returns to that state". A. Grahl-Madsen, "Protection of refugees by their country of origin", *Yale Journal of International Law* 11 (1986), 362-395, at 362.

44 Ibid., at 376.

45 See, in particular, the *Nationality Decrees Case* ((1923) PCIJ Ser. B, No. 4) and the *Lotus Case* (PCIJ Ser. A, No. 10), referred to in G. Goodwin-Gill, op. cit., *supra* note 5, at 4.

46 E.g., visa requirements for Bosnian refugees during the Bosnian conflict, accelerated procedures for nationals from "safe countries of origin" or who have passed through a "safe third country", persons granted temporary protection instead of refugee status because they are coming as a part of a mass influx.

47 T. Einarsen, "Discrimination and consequences for the position of aliens", *Nordic Journal of International Law* 64 (1995), at 441-446.

48 G. Goodwin-Gill, op. cit., *supra* note 5, 57, 195-197.

49 Article 1 (3) and Articles 55 and 56 of the United Nations Charter.

50 E.g., Article 2 of the UDHR 1948, Article 2 (1) of the ICCPR, Article 2 (2) ICESCR.

51 For a full account of the international law applicable to aliens, see James C. Hathaway, op. cit., *supra* note 5, 75-153.

52 In *Rasmussen v. Denmark*, judgment of 28 November 1984, the Court considered that since the list of grounds of discrimination in Article 14 was not exhaustive, it was not necessary to determine the basis for the different treatment between a husband and a wife. And in *Salgueiro da*

Silva Mouta, for instance, the Court applied Article 14 in relation to discrimination on the ground of sexual orientation (judgment of 21 December 1999).

53 Note that in the context of an alleged violation of Article 14 taken in conjunction with Article 1 of Protocol No. 1 (but also Articles 8 and 13 of the ECHR), the Court has usually declined to examine the claim under Article 14 if it has found a violation of Article 1 of Protocol No. 1 (and/or Articles 8 and 13 of the ECHR). E.g., *Cyprus v. Turkey* (2001) and *Eugenia Michaelidou Developments Ltd and Michael Tymvios v. Turkey*, judgment of 31 July 2003.

54 *Abdulaziz, Cabales and Balkandali v. the United Kingdom*, judgment of 28 May 1985, paragraphs 65, 71-72.

55 This observation is reinforced by the fact that it is a prerequisite to membership that "Every member of the Council of Europe must accept the principles of the rule of law and of the enjoyment by all persons within its jurisdiction of human rights and fundamental freedoms" (Article 3, Statute of the Council of Europe). This view is reiterated in Article 1 of the ECHR: "The High Contracting Parties shall secure to everyone within their jurisdiction the rights and freedoms" defined in the ECHR.

56 *Belgian Linguistic Case* (Merits), 34; and *Marckx v. Belgium*, judgment of 13 June 1979, paragraph 33.

57 *Supra* note 54, paragraphs 74-80.

58 Judgment of 30 September 2003, paragraph 49.

59 Judgment of 13 December 2005, paragraph 58.

60 *Supra* note 54, paragraph 72.

61 E.g., *Darby v. Sweden*, judgment of 23 October 1990, paragraph 33, where the Government did not argue that the distinction in treatment between resident and non-resident non-nationals for the purposes of a religious tax had a legitimate aim.

62 *Moustaquim v. Belgium*, judgment of 18 February 1991.

63 As of 28 June 2006, the only countries to have both signed and ratified Protocol No. 12 are: Albania, Armenia, Bosnia and Herzegovina, Croatia, Cyprus, Finland, Georgia, Luxembourg, Netherlands, San Marino, Serbia, "the former Yugoslav Republic of Macedonia" and Ukraine. Counties that have not even signed Protocol No. 12 are: Andorra, Bulgaria, Denmark, France, Lithuania, Malta, Monaco, Poland, Sweden, Switzerland and United Kingdom.

64 This protocol brings the ECHR closer to the ICCPR. In particular, Article 26 guarantees an "autonomous right" to freedom from discrimination "in law or in fact in any field regulated and protected by public authorities". See T. Einarsen, op. cit., *supra* note 47, at 434; Steiner and Alston, op. cit., *supra*, note 31, 788; G. Moon, "The draft discrimination protocol to the European Convention on Human Rights: a progress report", *European Human Rights Law Review* (1) 2000, 49-53.

65 Explanatory report to Protocol No. 12 notes that the extent of such positive obligations "is likely to be limited" because of the reference to the "enjoyment of any right set forth by law" in paragraph 1 of Article 1 and the reference to "by any public authority" in paragraph 2 of

Article 1. Explanatory report, paragraph 27, available at:
http://conventions.coe.int/Treaty/en/Reports/Html/177.htm

66 There is as yet no case law on Article 1 of Protocol No. 12.

67 1970, paragraph 34.

68 Article 12, EC Treaty, as amended by the Amsterdam Treaty.

69 Title IV of the EC Treaty, as amended by the Amsterdam Treaty.

70 *Belgian Linguistic case* and *Marckx*, op. cit., *supra* note 56.

71 H. Lambert, "Seeking asylum on gender grounds", *International Journal of Discrimination and the Law* 1 (2) 1995, 153-178.

72 R.B. Lillich, *The Human Rights of Aliens in Contemporary International Law* (1984), 94.

73 Article 16 reads as follows: "Nothing in Articles 10, 11 and 14 shall be regarded as preventing the High Contracting parties from imposing restrictions on the political activity of aliens."

74 *Collected edition of the "Travaux préparatoires" of the European Convention on Human Rights*, Vol. III (1976), 266. See also the Commission's statement in *Piermont v. France*, paragraph 58: "those who drafted [Article 16] were subscribing to a concept that was then prevalent in international law, under which a general, unlimited restriction of the political activities of aliens was thought legitimate".

75 R. Wallace, op. cit., *supra*, note 15, 51. Harris et al., op. cit., *supra* note 20, 508.

76 Judgment of 27 April 1995.

77 Ibid., paragraph 64.

78 Harris et al., op. cit., *supra* note 20, at 509. Judges Ryssdal, Matscher, Sir John Freeland and Jungwiert, in a joint partly dissenting opinion, criticised the lack of reasoning of the decision and found that Article 16 should have been regarded as having at least some relevance by the Court, since the applicant was clearly an alien in the eyes of French law, and therefore in the sense of Article 16. They did, however, add that though relevant, Article 16 did not grant states unfettered discretion; in particular they must respect the principle of proportionality.

79 E.g., confinement in an airport transit lounge and nearby hotel (*Amuur v. France*, judgment of 26 June 1996).

80 Outside the restrictions contained in Article 5 (1) *a-f,* states may derogate from the right to liberty and security "In time of war or other public emergency" (Article 15). The Court assesses the necessity of such derogations in a restrictive way. See, e.g., *Aksoy v. Turkey* (*supra* note 25): fourteen days in custody (and without judicial intervention) was held to be too long even during a state of emergency – although it did allow suspected terrorists to be held for up to seven days without judicial control in *Brannigan and McBride v. the United Kingdom* (judgment of 26 May 1993). See also *Çakici v. Turkey* (judgment of 8 July 1999): unacknowledged detention of at least three weeks violates Article 5 even in a state of emergency.

81 Exceptions to Article 5 (1) are not mutually exclusive (*Eriksen v. Norway*, judgment of 27 May 1997, paragraph 76). Thus an alien could be lawfully detained following a criminal conviction by a competent court (5 (1) a) pending deportation (5 (1) *f*).

82 *Supra* note 9.

83 Ibid., paragraph 42 (referring to *Guzzardi v. Italy*, judgment of 6 November 1980, paragraph 92).

84 Commission's report in *Agee v. the United Kingdom*, Application No. 7729/76, DR 7/164.

85 *Amuur, supra* note 79, paragraph 43.

86 Ibid., paragraph 50.

87 Ibid., paragraph 53.

88 *Winterwerp v. the Netherlands*, judgment of 24 October 1979, paragraphs 39 and 46.

89 *Amuur, supra* note 79, paragraph 43.

90 Judgment of 15 November 1996, paragraph 112. See also, *Čonka v. Belgium*, judgment of 5 February 2002, paragraph 38, and *Saadi v. the United Kingdom*, judgment of 11 July 2006, paragraph 44.

91 Detention should also be interrupted as soon as a decision has been made that deportation or extradition will not take place and grounds for further detention would have to be found elsewhere in Article 5 (1) *a-e*.

92 *Supra* note 90, paragraph 117.

93 Ibid., paragraph 122. However, the advisory panel was not found to provide sufficient safeguard under Article 5 (4) and Article 13 taken in conjunction with Article 3.

94 *Supra* note 90.

95 Ibid., paragraph 40.

96 Ibid., paragraphs 44-45.

97 See also Committee of Ministers of the Council of Europe, Recommendation No. R (94) 5 on guidelines to inspire practices of the member states of the Council of Europe concerning the arrival of asylum-seekers at European airports.

98 The requirement of promptness was found to be met by delays of seven hours (*Fox, Campbell and Hartley v. the United Kingdom*, judgment of 30 August 1990, paragraph 42) as well as two days (*Čonka v. Belgium, supra* note 90). But this requirement was not found to be met by a delay of seventy-six hours (*Saadi v. the United Kingdom, supra* note 90, paragraph 55), or four days (*Shamayev and Others v. Georgia and Russia*, paragraph 416), or ten days (*Van der Leer v. the Netherlands*, judgment of 21 February 1990, paragraph 31).

99 Application No. 9174/80, DR 40/42.

100 See generally, Harris et al., op. cit., *supra* note 20, 128-160. See also C. Giakoumopoulos, "Detention of asylum-seekers in the light of Article 5 of the European Convention on Human Rights", in *Detention of asylum-seekers in Europe: analysis and perspectives* (J. Hughes and F. Liebaut eds., 1998), 161-182.

101 *Supra* note 99.

102 *Sanchez-Reisse v. Switzerland*, judgment of 21 October 1986, paragraph 57: the right to seek judicial review must be an effective right, and *Hood v. the United Kingdom*, judgment of 18 February 1999, paragraph 69: it must also be an enforceable right.

103 *Chahal, supra* note 90, paragraph 127.

104 Ibid., paragraph 128.

105 Ibid., paragraph 131.

106 Ibid., paragraphs 132 and 130.

107 Judgment of 20 June 2002, paragraph 94.

108 E.g., in *De Wilde, Ooms and Versyp v. Belgium*, judgment of 18 June 1971, the Court found a violation of Article 5 (4) even though detention under Article 5 (1) was lawful.

109 See, however, the exceptional circumstances of the case *Çakici v. Turkey* (*supra* note 80) where the Court found a violation of Article 5, on the ground of the unacknowledged detention of the applicant's brother, and a violation of Article 13, on the ground of the applicant having been denied an effective remedy in respect of his brother's disappearance.

110 *Tsirlis and Kouloumpas v. Greece*, judgment of 29 May 1997.

111 N. Blake QC, Keynote speech, *Proceedings of the Second Colloquy on the European Convention on Human Rights and the protection of refugees, asylum-seekers and displaced persons*, Council of Europe, Strasbourg, 2000, 84. In *Gartukayev v. Russia*, the Court found a violation of Article 2 of Protocol No. 4 on the ground that the restriction on the applicant's right to liberty of movement had not been imposed "in accordance with the law" as required by Article 2, paragraphs 3 and 4 of Protocol No. 4 (judgment of 13 December 2005, paragraphs 21-22). See also, *Timishev v. Russia*, judgment of 13 December 2005, paragraphs 48-49.

112 N. Blake, op. cit., *supra* note 111.

113 The *travaux préparatoires* reveal that in the English version "lawfully" was preferred over "legally" and that in the French version, "*régulièrement*" was preferred over "*légalement*", to reflect the wide discretionary powers enjoyed by most administrative authorities to control the entry and residence of aliens. See, A. Drzemczewski, *The position of aliens in relation to the European Convention on Human Rights* (1984), 10.

114 Situation at 31 July 2006. Some states have further restricted the application of Article 2 of Protocol No. 4 by making certain reservations.

115 *P. v. the Federal Republic of Germany*, Application No. 12068/86, DR 51/237.

116 H.G. Schermers, "Human rights and free movement of persons: the role of the European Commission and Court of Human Rights", in Schermers et al. (eds.), *Free movement of persons – Legal problems and experiences* (1993), 238.

117 A. Drzemczewski, op. cit., *supra* note 113, 11. This is also the interpretation of "lawfully resident" given by the Commission in the context of Article 1 of Protocol No. 7 (see *infra*).

118 Application No. 7011/75, DR 4/215, at 235.

119 J.-M. Henckaerts, "The current status and content of the prohibition of mass expulsion of aliens", *Human Rights Law Journal* (15) 1994, 301.

120 *Alibaks and Others v. the Netherlands*, Application No. 14209/88, DR 59/274.

121 *Becker, supra* note 118, at 235.

122 E.g., *Andric v. Sweden*, decision of (in)admissibility of 23 February 1999, para. 1.

123 *Supra* note 98, paragraph 63.

124 Protocol No. 7 was adopted with the intention of bringing the protection afforded under the ECHR closer to that under the International Covenant on Civil and Political Rights, which provides a similar guarantee in its Article 13.

125 R. Cholewinski, op. cit., *supra* note 6, 398-399. Harris et al., op. cit., *supra* note 20, 565-566.

126 Application No. 19373/92, DR 74/199, at 209. See also, *S.T. v. France* (1993) and *Sejdovic and Sulejmanovic v. Italy* (2002).

127 See Explanatory memorandum to Protocol No. 7.

128 Article 1 (2). *Davies et al. c. la Roumanie* (2003). But see *Lupsa v. Romania,* Application No. 10337/04, judgment of 8 June 2006.

129 See *infra.*

130 *Supra* note 128.

131 Ibid., paragraph 53.

132 Ibid., paragraphs 55-57.

133 The scope of this provision could equally have been discussed as a qualified right under section 2.C. (*infra*), which is concerned with considerations of interpretation by the Strasbourg organs. However, I have chosen to deal with it here because Article 1 (1) expressly refers to the "general principles of international law" which only benefit aliens.

134 *Ilić v. Croatia,* Application No. 42389/98, decision of 19 September 2000.

135 *Oppenheim's*, op. cit., *supra* note 9, 910-927.

136 Judgment of 21 February 1986, paragraph 62. See also *Beaumartin v. France*, judgment of 24 November 1994. In the first edition of Human rights file No. 8 (op. cit., *supra* note 113, at 12), Drzemczewski quotes the following passage from a report prepared by the committee of experts from 18 July 1951:

"The Swedish Delegation pointed out – and requested that the fact be mentioned in these conclusions – that the general principles of international law referred to under Article 1 of the Protocol only applied to relations between a state and non-nationals.

At the request of the German and Belgian Delegations, it was agreed that the general principles of international law, in their present connotation, entailed the obligation to pay compensation to non-nationals in cases of expropriation."

137 P. van Dijk and G.J.H. van Hoof, *Theory and practice of the European Convention on Human Rights* (1998), 636.

138 Judgment of 5 January 2000, paragraph 110.

139 Ibid., paragraphs 120-121.

140 Judgment of 23 February 1995, paragraph 59.

141 Judgment of 24 October 1986, paragraph 51.

142 Y. Winisdoerffer, "Margin of appreciation and Article 1 of Protocol No. 1", *Human Rights Law Journal* (19) 1998, 18-20. Note that the Court has dealt with several cases involving the loss of control and enjoyment of property by displaced Greek Cypriots in Northern Cyprus (i.e., not aliens), see for instance, *Loizidou v. Turkey* (*supra* note 12) and *Cyprus v. Turkey* (*supra* note 31).

143 *Gaygusuz v. Austria,* judgment of 16 September 1996, and *Koua Poirrez v. France, supra* note 58.

144 *Janković v. Croatia,* (in)admissibility decision of 12 October 2000.

145 In contrast with Drzemczewski, I do not consider Articles 5 and 6 to constitute "minimum rights", mainly because I do not see the ECHR as guaranteeing a "hierarchy" of rights. Instead, I suggest that every right and freedom in the ECHR constitutes a "minimum right" in the sense that the ECHR provides a basic floor below which nobody is allowed to fall without violating the relevant standard. There is a separate question with regard to the applicability of these rights. In practice, some rights are recognised to be so fundamental as to call for absolute protection, while others are "defined in too general terms to be fully 'self-executing'." See H. Waldock, "The effectiveness of the system set up by the European Convention on Human Rights", *Human Rights Law Journal* 1 (1980), 1, at 9.

146 It has been argued that the notion of "absolute rights" does not exist, because every right may be said to be limited to some extent for reasons of contextual limitations (e.g., Article 3) or expressed limitations (e.g., Articles 8-11). While conceptually an interesting argument (as developed, e.g., by M. Addo and N. Grief in "Some practical issues affecting the notion of absolute right in Article 3 European Convention on Human Rights", *European Law Review* 23 (1998), 17-30, and in "Is there a policy behind the decisions and judgments relating to Article 3 of the European Convention on Human Rights?", *European Law Review* 20 (1995), 178) the distinction between absolute and qualified rights remains nevertheless valid and useful as a theoretical framework. Furthermore, some of the conclusions reached by Addo and Grief need to be revisited in light of recent judgments by the Court relating to Article 3, in particular *Selmouni v. France* (see G. Cohen-Jonathan, op. cit., *supra* note 29).

147 P. Mahoney, op. cit., *supra* note 33, 2.

148 Ibid.

149 R. Wallace, op. cit., *supra* note 15, 10-11 and 32-33.

150 E.g., *Jamil v. France,* judgment of 8 June 1995, in which the Court found a violation of Article 7 (1) in the case of a Brazilian national sentenced to imprisonment in France on grounds of prevention of drug trafficking.

151 *Supra* note 90, paragraph 79.

152 *Öcalan v. Turkey* (judgment of 12 May 2005) and *Ramzy v. the Netherlands* (pending, Application No. 25424/05). See also, Third Party Intervention Submissions by Liberty & Justice in *Ramzy v. the Netherlands*; and Written Comments by Amnesty International Ltd., The Association for the Prevention of Torture, Human Rights Watch, Interights, the International Commission of Jurists, Open Society Justice Initiative and Redress in *Ramzy v. the Netherlands.* See also, Observations of the governments of Lithuania, Portugal, Slovakia and the United Kingdom intervening in *Ramzy v the Netherlands,* arguing against the absolute nature of Article 3.

153 *Chahal v. the United Kingdom, supra* note 90, paragraph 105. See also the Report by the Council of Europe Commissioner for Human Rights (2005, paragraphs 12-13).

154 International law distinguishes between expulsion and extradition. Expulsion is an administrative measure in the form of a government order directing an alien to leave the territory; it is often used interchangeably

with deportation. Extradition is "the delivery of an accused or a convicted individual to the state where he is accused of, or has been convicted of a crime, by the state on whose territory he happens for the time to be". *Oppenheim's,* op. cit., *supra* note 9, 940-962. However, in the context of this study I shall use the word "expulsion" to mean any measure aiming at removing an alien from the territory in which s/he is present, i.e., deportation (including *reconduction à la frontière* – the accompanying of a person to the border of the expelling country), extradition and *refoulement.*

155 The case law shows that the Strasbourg organs have relied primarily on Article 3 to decide such cases. But see, e.g., *M.A.R. v. the United Kingdom* (admissibility decision of 16 January 1997): the Commission found admissible the complaint that the applicant's expulsion to Iran would constitute a violation of Article 2 because of a real risk of being sentenced to death there; *Tatete v. Switzerland* (judgment of 6 July 2000, friendly settlement): illegal immigrant suffering from Aids and claiming that sending her back to the Democratic Republic of the Congo would be in breach of Article 2; and *Köksal v. the Netherlands* (decision of 19 September 2000): a case of death of a Turkish national following ill-treatment during arrest and police custody declared admissible by the Commission under both Articles 2 and 3.

156 *T.I. v. the United Kingdom, supra* note 18. See also, e.g., *Soering v. the United Kingdom, supra* note 16, paragraph 91, and *Chahal v. the United Kingdom, supra* note 90, paragraph 80.

157 *Soering, supra* note 16, paragraph 91.

158 Ibid., paragraph 103. But see *M.A.R. v. the United Kingdom, supra* note 155, in which the Commission declared admissible under Article 2 an application on the ground that the applicant could face the death penalty if returned to Iran. Note also that for States Parties to Protocol No. 6 (the United Kingdom was not a party at that time), there would be a violation of this protocol in the event of such a person being expelled to a country where s/he would be subjected to a real and present risk of death penalty.

159 *Soering, supra* note 16, paragraph 111.

160 Ibid., paragraph 91.

161 *D. v. the United Kingdom, supra* note 14, paragraph 59. See also *Bahaddar v. the Netherlands,* Commission report (judgment of 19 February 1998), and *T.I. v. the United Kingdom, supra* note 18.

162 Note also that admissibility requirements are particularly stringent. For instance, in *Vijayanathan and Pusparajah v. France,* judgment of 27 August 1992, the Court failed to recognise the applicants as "victims" of a violation because no expulsion order had yet been made against them. See, H. Lambert, "Protection against *refoulement* from Europe: human rights law comes to the rescue", *International and Comparative Law Quarterly* 48 (1999), 515-544, at 523-530. However, the recent tendency seems to require less formalism. In particular, the Court considers the following as constituting exceptions to the admissibility criteria that all domestic remedies available must be exhausted: the existence of particular or special circumstances (e.g., *Akdivar and Others v. Turkey,* judgment of 16 September 1996, and *Aksoy v. Turkey, supra* note 25) and the ineffectiveness of an investigation into the

allegation of a violation of Article 3 (*Yaşa v. Turkey*, judgment of 2 September 1998 and *Selmouni v. France, supra* note 27). See G. Cohen-Jonathan, *supra* note 29, at 196-199.

163 *Vilvarajah and Others v. the United Kingdom*, judgment of 30 October 1991, paragraph 111.

164 *T.I. v. the United Kingdom, supra* note 18.

165 For cases involving national security, see, e.g., *Chahal v. the United Kingdom, supra* note 90 (successful case), *H.L.R. v. France*, judgment of 29 April 1997 (unsuccessful case) and *Cruz Varas and Others v. Sweden*, judgment of 20 March 1991 (unsuccessful case). See, generally, H. Lambert, "Protection against refoulement", op. cit., *supra* note 162, at 538-540. For cases involving public good, see *F.v. the United Kingdom*, (in)admissibility decision of 31 August 2004).

166 *Selcuk and Asker v. Turkey*, judgment of 24 April 1998, paragraphs 26 and 56.

167 *Soering, supra* note 16, paragraph 100.

168 *Supra* note 10, paragraph 167.

169 *Selmouni, supra* note 27, paragraphs 97-100.

170 Ibid., paragraph 101.

171 In terms of protection against ill-treatment in the event of an expulsion, it does not really matter whether Article 3 applies on the basis of torture or inhuman or degrading treatment, except perhaps that the Court will be more sympathetic towards a case of torture or death. However, outside expulsion cases, the difference between torture, inhuman and degrading treatment is mainly relevant for the Court in matters of compensation because the treatment has already occurred.

172 N. Blake, op. cit., *supra* note 111, at 83.

173 H. Lambert, "The European Convention on Human Rights and the protection of refugees: limits and opportunities", *Refugee Survey Quarterly* 24(2) 2005, at 41.

174 *Tyrer, supra* note 26, paragraphs 29-30. Thus, in *Jabari v. Turkey* the Court recognised that stoning for adultery in Iran constituted treatment contrary to Article 3 (judgment of 11 July 2000).

175 To read more on this issue, see H. Lambert, "The European Convention on Human Rights", *supra* note 173, at 41-43.

176 *B.B. v. France*, judgment of 7 September 1998.

177 *Karara v. Finland*, (in)admissibility decision of 29 May 1998.

178 Admissibility decision of 19 May 1994.

179 Friendly settlement of 4 July 1991.

180 *Supra* note 14. See also, e.g., *Ahmed v. Austria*, judgment of 17 December 1996 and *H.L.R. v. France, supra* note 165. It further follows from *D. v. the United Kingdom* (*supra,* note 14) but also, for instance, *H.L.R. v. France* (*supra* note 165) that the Court does not consider the source of the ill-treatment in the receiving country to be relevant to a determination under Article 3.

181 *Bensaid v. the United Kingdom*, judgment of 6 February 2001, paragraphs 38-40. See also *Arcila Henao v. the Netherlands* (inadmissibility decision of 24 June 2003), similar in facts to *D.* but declared inadmissible by the Court because the situation of the applicant although serious was not of an exceptional nature.

182 E.g., *Giama v. Belgium*, Application No. 7612/76, DR 21/73; *Harabi v. the Netherlands*, Application No. 10798/84, DR 46/112.

183 UNHCR's written submissions to the Court in *T.I. v. the United Kingdom* (*supra* note 18). See also Swiss Delegation of the CAHAR, "Obligations incumbent on states under public international law with respect to the readmission of their own nationals and aliens", CAHAR (96) 12, Council of Europe (1996), 1-44.

184 London, 30 November-1 December 1992.

185 Council Directive 2005/85/EC of 1 December 2005, OJ 13 December 2005, L 326/13-34 on minimum standards on procedures in member states for granting and withdrawing refugee status (Article 27).

186 *Supra* note 18. The case was nevertheless declared inadmissible by the Court on the facts of it.

187 *Bosphorus Hava Yollari Turizm Ve Ticaret Anonim Şirketi (Bosphorus Airways) v. Ireland*, judgment of 30 June 2005.

188 E.g., *Brückmann v. the Federal Republic of Germany*, Application No. 6242/73, DR 46/202. Refer also to *D. v. the United Kingdom* (*supra* note 14), in its narrowest interpretation (paragraph 53).

189 *Nsona v. the Netherlands* (judgment of 28 November 1996).

190 *Öcalan v. Turkey, supra* note 152, paragraph 184.

191 7th General Report (CPT/Inf(97)10) and 13th General Report (CPT/Inf (2003)35).

192 Article 5 (1) *c* and *f.*

193 Judgment of 15 July 2002, paragraph 95.

194 See also *Peers v. Greece*, judgment of 19 April 2001, paras. 67-68 and 74, and *Price v. the United Kingdom*, judgment of 10 July 2001, paras. 23 and 30.

195 E.g., 7th General Report (CPT/Inf(97)10).

196 *Iorgov v. Bulgaria*, judgment of 11 March 2004, paragraph 83.

197 *Öcalan v. Turkey, supra* note 152, paragraph 192.

198 Judgment of 4 December 1995, paragraph 38.

199 *Supra* note 194.

200 *Mouisel v France*, judgment of 14 November 2002, paragraphs 40 and 43.

201 *Toteva v. Bulgaria*, judgment of 19 May 2004.

202 This convention entered into force on 1 February 1989 following the required seven ratifications.

203 See Article 1 of the text of the CPT, and Explanatory memorandum. For more details on the work of the CPT, refer to its annual General Reports of activities. See also, e.g., A. Cassesse, "A new approach to human rights: the European Convention for the Prevention of Torture", *American Journal of International Law* 83 (1989), 128-153; M. Evans and R. Morgan, "The European Convention for the Prevention of Torture: 1992-1997", *International and Comparative Law Quarterly* 46 (1997), 663-675.

204 *Aerts v. Belgium*, judgment of 30 July 1998.

205 This rule is the same as the old Rule 36 provided under the Rules of Procedures of the European Commission of Human Rights.

206 H. Lambert, "Protection against refoulement", op. cit., *supra* note 162, at 530-532.

207 Ibid.

208 *Mamatkulov and Abdurasulovic v. Turkey*, judgment of 6 February 2003. See also, Olivier de Schutter, "The binding character of the provisional measures adopted by the European Court of Human Rights", *International Law FORUM du droit international* 7 (2005), 16-23.

209 E.g., *Chahal, supra* note 90.

210 E.g., *Ahmed, supra* note 180.

211 See, e.g., separate opinion of Mr Cabral Barreto to the European Commission of Human Rights' report on the case *B.B. v. France* (*supra* note 176), criticising the Court's approach. Unlike the European Court of Human Rights, the Inter-American Court of Human Rights has often declared injunctions against a violator state. See G. Cohen-Jonathan, op. cit., *supra* note 29, at 200, note 35.

212 E.g., *Paez v. Sweden*, judgment of 30 October 1997, *B.B. v. France, supra* note 176, *Abdurahim Incedursun v. the Netherlands*, judgment of 22 June 1999, *Tatete v. Switzerland, supra* note 155. See also, Resolution ResDH (2005)115 concerning the judgment of the European Court of Human Rights of 8 November 2002 (friendly settlement) in the case of *Sulejmanovic and Others and Sejdovic and Sulejmanovic against Italy* (adopted by the Committee of Ministers on 14 December 2005 at the 948th meeting of the Ministers' Deputies.

213 Council Directive 2004/83/EC of 29 April 2004, OJ 30 September 2004, L 304/12-23 on minimum standards for the qualification and status of third country nationals as refugees and persons otherwise in need of international protection and the content of the protection granted.

214 *Tugar v. Italy*, (in)admissibility decision of 18 October 1995.

215 Judgment of 28 October 1998, 3124.

216 *R v. Secretary of State for the Home Department*, ex parte *Adam, Limbuela and Tesema*, House of Lords, judgment of 3 November 2005, available at http://www.publications.parliament.uk/pa/ld/ldjudgmt.htm

217 *Pancenko v. Latvia*, (in)admissibility decision of 28 October 1999. See also Separate Opinion of Mr Cabral Barreto to the Commission's report in *B.B. v. France* (*supra* note 176), and A. Cassese, "Can the notion of inhuman and degrading treatment be applied to socio-economic conditions?", *European Journal of International Law* 2(2) 1999.

218 (In)admissibility decision of 6 March 1978.

219 *Supra* note 54. See also, more recently *Cyprus v. Turkey, supra* note 31, paragraphs 306-398.

220 Harris et al., op. cit., *supra* note 20, at 82.

221 Ibid., 83.4.

222 *Kalderas Gypsies v. the Federal Republic of Germany and the Netherlands*, Application Nos. 7823-7824/77, DR 11/221.

223 E.g., *Selmouni, supra* note 27. See, G. Cohen-Jonathan, *supra* note 29, 181-203.

224 *Selmouni, supra* note 27, paragraph 79. See also, previously, *Kurt v. Turkey*, judgment of 25 May 1998, *Chahal, supra* note 90, and *McCann and Others v. the United Kingdom*, judgment of 27 September 1995.

225 Judgment of 28 October 1998

226 Ibid., para. 92, referring to *Ribitsch v. Austria* (judgment of 4 December 1995). This implied duty of investigation was confirmed, for instance, in *Sevtap Veznedarolu v. Turkey* (judgment of 11 April 2000) and *Ipek v. Turkey* (judgment of 17 February 2004).

227 See also, for instance, *Dikme v. Turkey* (judgment of 11 July 2000) and *Jabari v. Turkey* (*supra* note 174).

228 On the relationship between the procedural guarantees under Article 3 and Article 13 and in particular the overlap between the implied state's duty under Article 3 and that under Article 13, see H. Lambert, "The European Convention on Human Rights", *supra* note 173, at 46-49.

229 Judgment of 27 June 2000, paragraph 92.

230 To read more on this issue, see H. Lambert, "The European Convention on Human Rights", op. cit., *supra* note 173, at 46-49.

231 Note also that in other contexts, such as detention, Article 5 provides more stringent procedural obligations for states to guarantee a remedy. A. Drzemczewski and C. Giakoumopoulos, "Article 13", in *La Convention européenne des Droits de l'Homme* (Decaux, Imbert, Petiti, eds., 1995), 455-474.

232 E.g., *Selçuk and Asker v. Turkey, supra* note 166.

233 *Boyle and Rice*, judgment of 27 April 1988, paragraph 52; referred to, for instance, in *Soering* (*supra* note 16, paragraph 120). The Court does not require incorporation of the ECHR into domestic law. However, as remarked by Judges De Meyer and Pettiti, "The object and purpose of the European Convention on Human Rights was not to create, but to recognise rights which must be respected and protected even in the absence of any instrument of positive law. It has to be accepted that, everywhere in Europe, these rights 'bind the legislature, the executive and the judiciary, as directly applicable law' and as 'supreme law of the land'." Separate opinion, *The* Observer *and* Guardian *Case*, judgment of 26 November 1991.

234 Note that Article 5 has its own procedural guarantee proviso. However, Article 13 remains relevant because the content of Article 13 is wider than the requirement for an investigation under Article 5. E.g., *Kurt v. Turkey* (*supra* note 224), paragraph 140.

235 *Klass and Others v. the Federal Republic of Germany*, judgment of 6 September 1978, paragraph 64. Van Dijk and Van Hoof, *supra* note 137, 698.

236 *Silver v. the United Kingdom*, judgment of 25 March 1983, paragraph 113. *Boyle and Rice, supra* note 233, paragraph 52.

237 *Powell and Rayner v. the United Kingdom*, judgment of 21 February 1990, paragraph 33.

238 *Silver and Others v. the United Kingdom, supra* note 236, paragraph 113. See also Recommendation No. (98) 13 of the Committee of Ministers of the Council of Europe on the right of rejected asylum seekers to an effective remedy against decisions on expulsion in the context of Article 3 of the ECHR.

239 *Silver and Others v. United Kingdom, supra* note 236, paragraph 113. See also *Leander v. Sweden*, judgment of 26 March 1987, paras. 29-30, and *Klass, supra* note 235, paragraph 67.

240 Judgment of 25 September 1997, paragraph 107.

241 *Supra* note 90, paragraph 151.

242 Ibid., paragraph 153. See also, e.g., *Smith and Grady v. the United Kingdom*, judgment of 27 September 1999: judicial review does not provide effective remedy. In cases not involving national security, the Court has nevertheless been willing to regard judicial review as adequate remedy under Article 13 in cases involving the United Kingdom (e.g., *D. v. the United Kingdom, supra* note 14, paragraph 70 referring to *Soering v. the United Kingdom, supra* note 16, and to *Vilvarajah v. the United Kingdom, supra* note 163) but not in the case of Turkey (e.g., *Jabari v. Turkey, supra* note 174).

243 *Supra* note 174, paragaph 40.

244 Ibid., paragraph 49. See also *Riener v. Bulgaria*, for the finding of a violation of Article 13 in conjunction with Article 2 of Protocol No. 4 and Article 8 of the ECHR (judgment of 23 May 2006, paragraphs 135-143.

245 Commission's report on *Plattform "Ärzte für das Leben" v. Austria*, judgment of 21 June 1988. See also Recommendation No. R 98 (13) of the Committee of Ministers of the Council of Europe, Explanatory memorandum, para. 16. In this regard, the denial to asylum-seekers of the right to legal assistance or the right to basic subsistence could be in violation of Article 13, in conjunction with Article 3, by preventing the asylum seeker from appealing. See judgment by the Court of Appeal in the United Kingdom, *R v. Secretary of State for Social Security*, ex parte *Re B and Joint Council for the Welfare of Immigrants (JCWI)*, [1997] 1 WLR 275.

246 *Soering v. the United Kingdom, supra* note 16, paragraph 123. Confirmed, e.g., in *Vilvarajah v. the United Kingdom, supra* note 163, and *D. v. the United Kingdom, supra* note 14.

247 Judgment of 5 February 2002, paragraphs 81-83.

248 Conduct may nevertheless be relevant under Article 13.

249 N. Blake, op. cit., *supra* note 111, 78-90.

250 J. Cooper and T. de la Mare, "Bringing and defending a case under the Human Rights Act 1998", Bracton Law Lecture, University of Exeter, 26 October 2000.

251 My discussion on Article 8 is largely based on the following two publications: H. Lambert, "The European Convention on Human Rights and the right of refugees and other persons in need of protection to family reunification", Council of Europe, CAHAR (99) 1, and H. Lambert, "The European Court of Human Rights and the right of refugees and other persons in need of protection to family reunion", *International Journal of Refugee Law* 11 (3) (1999), 427-450. See also Committee of Ministers of the Council of Europe, Recommendation No. R (99) 23 on family reunion for refugees and other persons in need of international protection.

252 *Abdulaziz, Cabales and Balkandali v. the United Kingdom, supra* note 54.

253 *Gül v. Switzerland*, judgment of 19 February 1996. See also, e.g., *Nsona v. the Netherlands*, judgment of 28 November 1996 and *Ahmut v. the Netherlands*, judgment of 28 November 1996.

254 Judgment of 21 June 1988.

255 *Supra* note 62. See also *Beldjoudi v. France*, judgment of 26 March 1992; *Bouchelkia v. France*, judgment of 29 January 1997; and *Boujlifa v. France*, judgment of 21 October 1997.

256 *Mehemi v. France*, judgment of 26 September 1997, and *El Boujaïdi v. France*, judgment of 26 September 1997.

257 *Gül, supra* note 253, paragraph 38, first held in *Abdulaziz, Cabales and Balkandali v. the United Kingdom, supra* note 54, paragraph 68.

258 *Gül, supra* note 253, paragraph 38.

259 Concurring opinion by Judge Pettiti in *Nasri v. France*, judgment of 13 July 1995.

260 E.g., *Moustaquim v. Belgium, supra* note 62, paragraphs 46-47, and *Beldjoudi v. France, supra* note 255, paragraphs 79-80.

261 In the context of family reunion, the court has recognised that family life between parents and children does not cease following the divorce of a married couple (e.g., *Berrehab v. the Netherlands, supra* note 254), nor does it cease as a result of living apart (e.g., *Moustaquim v. Belgium, supra* note 62).

262 M.E. Mas, "La protection des enfants mineurs en Europe", 4 *Bulletin des droits de l'homme* 1995, 30-41.

263 *Nsona, supra* note 253. This reasoning is consistent with the Court's decisions in cases involving nationals where it has long recognised the existence of family life between near relatives. See, *Marckx, supra* note 56.

264 Judgment of 7 August 1996, paragraph 25, in which the Court referred to its judgment in *Niemietz v. Germany*, judgment of 16 December 1992. This judgment was confirmed in, e.g., *Bouchelkia, supra* note 255, and *Mehemi, supra* note 256.

265 Judgment of 9 October 2003, paragraphs 96-97.

266 *Gül, supra* note 253, paragraph 38. First stated in *Abdulaziz, supra* note 54, paragraph 67.

267 E.g., *Cruz Varas and Others v. Sweden, supra* note 165. See also *Nsona, supra* note 253, where the Court found no interference with the right to respect for family life because the state could not be blamed for the applicants' deceitful act regarding the identity of the 9 year old child.

268 See, e.g., *Abdulaziz, supra* note 54, *Gül, supra* note 253, *Ahmut, supra* note 253, and *Nsona, supra* note 253. Note, however, that in both *Gül* and *Ahmut*, the Commission reported an interference.

269 E.g., *Vijayanathan and Pusparajah v. France, supra* note 162, *Sen v. the Netherlands* (judgment of 21 December 2001) and *Rodrigues Da Silva and Hoogkamer v. the Netherlands* (judgment of 31 January 2006)

270 E.g., *Berrehab, supra* note 254, paragraph 23, *Moustaquim, supra* note 62, paragraph 36, *Ciliz v. the Netherlands*, judgment of 11 July 2000, paragraphs 66-72, and *Slivenko v. Latvia, supra* note 265, paragraphs 113-129.

271 See Storey's reference to the "elsewhere" approach and the "connections" approach, in H. Storey, "The right to family life and immigration case law at Strasbourg", *International and Comparative Law Quarterly* 39 (1990), at 329-330.

272 This requirement was successfully challenged by aliens in only two cases so far: *Al-Nashif v. Bulgaria*, judgment of 20 June 2002 (paragraphs

119, 121-124), and *Lupsa v. Romania*, judgment of 8 June 2006 (paragraphs 32-38). In both cases, the applicants had been deported on grounds of national security.

273 E.g., *Abdulaziz, supra* note 54, paragraph 67, and *Berrehab, supra* note 254, paragraphs 28-29. Note that in cases of entry, the Court tends to carry out the balance when determining the existence of an interference, and where no obstacles exist in developing normal family life elsewhere, the applicant is usually expected to return there.

274 *Beldjoudi, supra* note 255, paragraph 75.

275 For a recent illustration of this approach, see *Radovanovic v. Austria*, judgment of 22 April 2004.

276 *Nasri, supra* note 259 (about thirty years in France); *Boughanemi*, judgment of 24 April 1996 (twenty years in France), and *Chorfi, supra* note 264 (twenty-five years in Belgium).

277 As successfully demonstrated in *Beldjoudi, supra* note 255, and *Mehemi, supra* note 256, but not in *Boughanemi, supra* note 276, nor in *Chorfi, supra* note 264.

278 See *Moustaquim, supra* note 62 (147 offences committed but at a time when Mr Moustaquim was a minor, so deportation measure was found to be disproportionate) and compare it with *Chorfi, supra* note 264 (drug offence was found to be serious enough to justify interference) and *Bouchelkia, supra* note 255 (rape with violence and theft was found to be grave enough to justify interference).

279 *Moustaquim, supra* note 62, *Berrehab, supra* note 254, and *Radovanovic, supra* note 275.

280 E. Corouge, "Expulsion des étrangers et Article 8 de la Convention européenne des droits de l'homme", *Revue française de Droit administratif* 13 (2) (1997), 320.

281 See, e.g., *Bouchelkia, supra* note 255, *Mehemi, supra* note 256, *Nasri, supra*, note 259, and *Radovanovic, supra* note 275

282 See, e.g., *Boughanemi, supra* note 276, and *Chorfi, supra* note 264. Note that on 23 February 2001, the Parliamentary Assembly's Committee on Migration, Refugees and Demography called for such expulsion to take place only in "highly exceptional cases" because it considers such a measure to be "disproportionate and discriminatory" (Doc. 8986; see http://stars.coe.int).

283 E.g., *Chahal, supra* note 90, *D., supra* note 14, and *N. v. Finland*, judgment of 26 July 2005.

284 E.g., *Gül, supra* note 253, and *Nsona, supra* note 253.

285 It may nonetheless be observed that in the very particular situation of Greek Cypriots displaced from northern Cyprus, the Court recognised a violation of Article 8 on the grounds that these displaced persons had been/were denied, amongst other rights, their right to family reunification (in particular, certain restrictions applied to the visits of children to their parents still living in the north) as a matter of policy and in the absence of any legal basis). *Cyprus v. Turkey, supra* note 31, paras. 292-293.

286 *Supra* note 181.

287 Ibid., paragraph 46.

288 Ibid., paragraph 47.

289 As in *D. v. the United Kingdom, supra* note 14.

290 Note that such a right was recently recognised by the House of Lords in *R (on the application of Razgar) v. SSHD*, 17 June 2004.

291 *Agee v. the United Kingdom, supra* note 84.

292 Note also that "Article 9 of the ECHR … guarantees to everyone the 'right to freedom of thought, conscience and religion', but … does not specify the provision of positive assistance to promote or facilitate this right". R. Cholewinski, op. cit., *supra* note 6, at 367.

293 Ibid., at 375.

294 *Piermont, supra* note 76, paragraph 78.

295 *Cyprus v. Turkey, supra* note 31, paragraph 245.

296 Ibid., paragraph 254.

297 Ibid., paragraph. 260.

298 Thus in *Abdulaziz, supra* note 54, the right of the applicants to enter and establish in the United Kingdom in order to join their wives settled in the United Kingdom had not been argued on the basis of Article 12 but of Articles 8 and 14.

299 See, Harris et al., op. cit., *supra* note 20, 440 (n.16) and 435-436, referring to the Commission's decision in *X v. the United Kingdom*, Application No. 6564/74, (in)admissibility decision of 21 May 1975.

300 *X v. the Netherlands*, Application No. 8896/80, (in)admissibility decision of 10 March 1981. See also, *X and Y v. the United Kingdom*, Application No. 7229/75, (in)admissibility decision of 15 December 1977.

301 *Leyla Şahin v. Turkey*, judgment of 10 November 2005, paragraph 141.

302 Ibid., paragraphs 137-138, referring to *Belgian Linguistic Case*, judgment of 23 July 1968, paragraph 22. For a recent example of this provision being applied successfully to entry into a university degree, see *Mürsel Eren v. Turkey*, judgment of 7 February 2006.

303 *Leyla Şahin v. Turkey, supra* note 301, paragraph 152.

304 *Belgian Linguistic Case, supra* note 302, paragraph 5.

305 *Leyla Şahin v. Turkey, supra* note 301, paragraph 154.

306 *Belgian Linguistic Case, supra* note 302, paragraph 5. Unlike under Articles 8 to 11 ECHR, however, the Court is not bound by an exhaustive list of "legitimate aims" when considering the use made by states of their discretion in this area.

307 Ibid.

308 Judgment of 13 December 2005, paragraph 64.

309 Referring to *Leyla Şahin v. Turkey, supra* note 301.

310 *Timishev v. Russia, supra* note 308, paragraph 32. Van Dijk and Van Hoof argue that at least as far as elementary education is concerned, Article 2 should be interpreted as to include the state duty "to create additional facilities within the existing education institutions for the benefit of those aliens having taken up residence in the territory for a considerable time who do not yet have sufficient command of the language in which education is conducted; otherwise the right to education will remain illusory for them for a long time". They further

question the extent to which aliens "without a residence permit can derive from this provision a right to education". Again they maintain that at least with regards to elementary education, they should be recognised "equal access to existing educational institutions", especially in cases where they have been authorised to remain on humanitarian grounds for an indefinite period of time. Van Dijk and Van Hoof, op. cit., *supra* note 137, at 654.

311 This guarantee aims at safeguarding the possibility of pluralism in education, an essential element in the preservation of the "democratic society" as conceived by the ECHR. *Efstratiou v. Greece*, judgment of 18 December 1996.

312 Harris et al., op. cit., *supra* note 20, at 548.

313 Van Dijk and Van Hoof, op. cit., *supra* note 137, 645.

314 Under the auspices of the Council of Europe, these standards are provided in the European Social Charter, the European Convention on Establishment, and the European Convention on the Legal Status of Migrant Workers. See Cholewinski, op. cit., *supra* note 6, 359-361.

315 Application No. 7671/76, (in)admissibility decision of 19 May 1977.

316 Ibid. See also more recently *Fadele v. the United Kingdom* (*supra*, note 179) declared admissible by the Commission. The dispute was the subject of a friendly settlement.

317 *Church of X v. the United Kingdom*, Application No. 3798/68, (in)admissibility decision of 17 December 1968.

318 *Supra*, section 1.B.

319 Judgment of 23 May 2006, paragraph 122.

320 Application No. 6779/74 (unpublished).

321 Outside the scope of immigration, i.e., in civil or criminal procedures, there is nothing in the Strasbourg case law to suggest that Article 6 would apply differently to nationals and aliens. See, e.g., *Biba v. Greece* (judgment of 26 September 2000), where the Court recognised a violation of Article 6 (1) combined with Article 6 (3) *c* in a case of criminal proceedings. The case involved an illegal immigrant from Albania who was found guilty of murder, theft with violence and illegal stay in Greece, and who was condemned to life imprisonment on the ground that he had no means of subsistence. Yet, he was refused free legal aid to lodge an appeal in the Court of Cassation.

322 *Supra* note 16.

323 Ibid., paragraph 115.

324 Judgment of 26 June 1992, paragraph 110. This case involved a national from Spain and a national from Czechoslovakia, both sentenced to fourteen years' imprisonment in France following a conviction for armed robbery.

325 *Supra* note 155.

326 E.g., *Farmakopoulos v. Belgium*, Application No. 11683/85, decision of 27 March 1992 (Article 6 does not apply to extradition proceedings), *X, Y, Z, V and W v. the United Kingdom*, Application No. 3325/67, decision of 15 December 1967 (entry); *V. P. v. the United Kingdom*, Application No. 13162/87, decision of 9 November 1987 (asylum); *Agee v. the United Kingdom, supra* note 84 (deportation).

327 Decision of 22 March 2000.

328 Judgment of 5 October 2000.

329 Ibid., paragraphs 37-38. However, as pointed out by Judges Loucaides and Traja in their dissenting opinion, "Article 1 of Protocol No. 7 was aimed at the establishment of a protection vis-à-vis the administration which in any case could not serve as a substitute for the judicial guarantees of Article 6 or even minimise the negative effects resulting from the absence of the latter. The protection in question may very well be supplementary to the judicial guarantees of Article 6."

330 Ibid., paragraph 39.

331 See *Feldbrugge v. the Netherlands*, judgment of 29 May 1986, and *Francesco Lombardo v. Italy*, judgment of 26 November 1992.

Sales agents for publications of the Council of Europe
Agents de vente des publications du Conseil de l'Europe

BELGIUM/BELGIQUE
La Librairie Européenne -
The European Bookshop
Rue de l'Orme, 1
B-1040 BRUXELLES
Tel.: +32 (0)2 231 04 35
Fax: +32 (0)2 735 08 60
E-mail: order@libeurop.be
http://www.libeurop.be

Jean De Lannoy
Avenue du Roi 202 Koningslaan
B-1190 BRUXELLES
Tel.: +32 (0)2 538 43 08
Fax: +32 (0)2 538 08 41
E-mail: jean.de.lannoy@dl-servi.com
http://www.jean-de-lannoy.be

**CANADA and UNITED STATES/
CANADA et ÉTATS-UNIS**
Renouf Publishing Co. Ltd.
1-5369 Canotek Road
OTTAWA, Ontario K1J 9J3, Canada
Tel.: +1 613 745 2665
Fax: +1 613 745 7660
Toll-Free Tel.: (866) 767-6766
E-mail: orders@renoufbooks.com
http://www.renoufbooks.com

**CZECH REPUBLIC/
RÉPUBLIQUE TCHÈQUE**
Suweco CZ, s.r.o.
Klecakova 347
CZ-180 21 PRAHA 9
Tel.: +420 2 424 59 204
Fax: +420 2 848 21 646
E-mail: import@suweco.cz
http://www.suweco.cz

DENMARK/DANEMARK
GAD
Vimmelskaftet 32
DK-1161 KØBENHAVN K
Tel.: +45 77 66 60 00
Fax: +45 77 66 60 01
E-mail: gad@gad.dk
http://www.gad.dk

FINLAND/FINLANDE
Akateeminen Kirjakauppa
PO Box 128
Keskuskatu 1
FIN-00100 HELSINKI
Tel.: +358 (0)9 121 4430
Fax: +358 (0)9 121 4242
E-mail: akatilaus@akateeminen.com
http://www.akateeminen.com

FRANCE
La Documentation française
(diffusion/distribution France entière)
124, rue Henri Barbusse
F-93308 AUBERVILLIERS CEDEX
Tél.: +33 (0)1 40 15 70 00
Fax: +33 (0)1 40 15 68 00
E-mail: prof@ladocumentationfrancaise.fr
http://www.ladocumentationfrancaise.fr

Librairie Kléber
1 rue des Francs Bourgeois
F-67000 STRASBOURG
Tel.: +33 (0)3 88 15 78 88
Fax: +33 (0)3 88 15 78 80
E-mail: francois.wolfermann@librairie-kleber.fr
http://www.librairie-kleber.com

**GERMANY/ALLEMAGNE
AUSTRIA/AUTRICHE**
UNO Verlag GmbH
August-Bebel-Allee 6
D-53175 BONN
Tel.: +49 (0)228 94 90 20
Fax: +49 (0)228 94 90 222
E-mail: bestellung@uno-verlag.de
http://www.uno-verlag.de

GREECE/GRÈCE
Librairie Kauffmann s.a.
Stadiou 28
GR-105 64 ATHINAI
Tel.: +30 210 32 55 321
Fax.: +30 210 32 30 320
E-mail: ord@otenet.gr
http://www.kauffmann.gr

HUNGARY/HONGRIE
Euro Info Service kft.
1137 Bp. Szent István krt. 12.
H-1137 BUDAPEST
Tel.: +36 (06)1 329 2170
Fax: +36 (06)1 349 2053
E-mail: euroinfo@euroinfo.hu
http://www.euroinfo.hu

ITALY/ITALIE
Licosa SpA
Via Duca di Calabria, 1/1
I-50125 FIRENZE
Tel.: +39 0556 483215
Fax: +39 0556 41257
E-mail: licosa@licosa.com
http://www.licosa.com

MEXICO/MEXIQUE
Mundi-Prensa México, S.A. De C.V.
Río Pánuco, 141 Delegacíon Cuauhtémoc
06500 MÉXICO, D.F.
Tel.: +52 (01)55 55 33 56 58
Fax: +52 (01)55 55 14 67 99
E-mail: mundiprensa@mundiprensa.com.mx
http://www.mundiprensa.com.mx

NETHERLANDS/PAYS-BAS
De Lindeboom Internationale Publicaties b.v.
M.A. de Ruyterstraat 20 A
NL-7482 BZ HAAKSBERGEN
Tel.: +31 (0)53 5740004
Fax: +31 (0)53 5729296
E-mail: books@delindeboom.com
http://www.delindeboom.com

NORWAY/NORVÈGE
Akademika
Postboks 84 Blindern
N-0314 OSLO
Tel.: +47 2 218 8100
Fax: +47 2 218 8103
E-mail: support@akademika.no
http://akademika.no

POLAND/POLOGNE
Ars Polona JSC
25 Obroncow Street
PL-03-933 WARSZAWA
Tel.: +48 (0)22 509 86 00
Fax: +48 (0)22 509 86 10
E-mail: arspolona@arspolona.com.pl
http://www.arspolona.com.pl

PORTUGAL
Livraria Portugal
(Dias & Andrade, Lda.)
Rua do Carmo, 70
P-1200-094 LISBOA
Tel.: +351 21 347 42 82 / 85
Fax: +351 21 347 02 64
E-mail: info@livrariaportugal.pt
http://www.livrariaportugal.pt

**RUSSIAN FEDERATION/
FÉDÉRATION DE RUSSIE**
Ves Mir
9a, Kolpacnhyi per.
RU-101000 MOSCOW
Tel.: +7 (8)495 623 6839
Fax: +7 (8)495 625 4269
E-mail: zimarin@vesmirbooks.ru
http://www.vesmirbooks.ru

SPAIN/ESPAGNE
Mundi-Prensa Libros, s.a.
Castelló, 37
E-28001 MADRID
Tel.: +34 914 36 37 00
Fax: +34 915 75 39 98
E-mail: liberia@mundiprensa.es
http://www.mundiprensa.com

SWITZERLAND/SUISSE
Van Diermen Editions – ADECO
Chemin du Lacuez 41
CH-1807 BLONAY
Tel.: +41 (0)21 943 26 73
Fax: +41 (0)21 943 36 05
E-mail: info@adeco.org
http://www.adeco.org

UNITED KINGDOM/ROYAUME-UNI
The Stationery Office Ltd
PO Box 29
GB-NORWICH NR3 1GN
Tel.: +44 (0)870 600 5522
Fax: +44 (0)870 600 5533
E-mail: book.enquiries@tso.co.uk
http://www.tsoshop.co.uk

**UNITED STATES and CANADA/
ÉTATS-UNIS et CANADA**
Manhattan Publishing Company
468 Albany Post Road
CROTTON-ON-HUDSON, NY 10520, USA
Tel.: +1 914 271 5194
Fax: +1 914 271 5856
E-mail: Info@manhattanpublishing.com
http://www.manhattanpublishing.com

Council of Europe Publishing/Editions du Conseil de l'Europe
F-67075 Strasbourg Cedex
Tel.: +33 (0)3 88 41 25 81 – Fax: +33 (0)3 88 41 39 10 – E-mail: publishing@coe.int – Website: http://book.coe.int